THE BILLY FIDGET LETTERS

NICK BATTLE
AND
ERIC DELVE

HODDER

First published in Great Britain in 2011 by Hodder & Stoughton
An Hachette UK company
This paperback edition first published in 2012

1

A CIP catalogue record for this title is available from the British Library

ISBN 978 0 340 99630 0
Ebook ISBN 978 1 444 70284 2

Typeset in Scala by Hewer Text UK Ltd, Edinburgh
Printed and bound in the UK by Clays Ltd, St Ives plc

Hodder & Stoughton policy is to use papers that are natural, renewable
and recyclable products and made from wood grown in sustainable
forests. The logging and manufacturing processes are expected to
conform to the environmental regulations of the country of origin.

Hodder & Stoughton Ltd
338 Euston Road
London NW1 3BH

www.hodderfaith.com

For Wendy Grisham
With love from
Nick and Eric

Dear God,

Are you there? It's me ... er ... William Fidget ... you remember, don't you?

I was the one who'd always drop his hymn book on the floor at St Ethelred's so I could have a peek at what the choirmistress was wearing. She was all lace and frills and kept my young heart pulsing (as well as other parts of my teenage anatomy) ... Celia Trollope, I think her name was ... anyway, I digress. Setting that aside (and as sins go it's not *that* big, is it? I was only thirteen), setting that aside, as I say, I was just wondering if you were available at the moment, as I'm in a bit of a pickle.

Actually that's a bit of an understatement. I'm drowning in brown stuff, and Branston's it isn't.

Can you help me, God? Are you there? Please?

Yours hopefully

William Fidget

Dear God,

It's me again. William. I know they say, 'A week is a long time in politics', but it's been ten days since I wrote to you so I hope that's OK. I know you must be *incredibly* busy but I'm in dire need of a word or two. God? You are there, aren't you?

Yours truly

William

Come on, God! If you're everything you're cracked up to be, at least give me some small sign! Even if you tell me to naff off at least I'll know you exist . . .

William

Dear Billy (well, you did ask whether I remembered you!),

Good to hear from you. I always like it when my old acquaintances get in touch.

But I hope you will not mind my saying that I prefer it when people are more direct. You reminded me of your interest in the choirmistress. You are quite right: as sins go, it wasn't enormous but your commitment to that particular kind of sin has been truly wholehearted, and seems to have got you into trouble throughout your life.

Here you can help me best: I know you are in lots of trouble, but when you mention being 'in a bit of a pickle', it would be more helpful if you could be direct about which part of the pickle you are referring to. 'Drowning in brown stuff' describes your situation pretty well. But which particular stream of effluent are you actually drowning in at the moment?

Yes, I know you're going to say: 'But you are God, surely you know?' In this kind of conversation, though, what I *know* is nowhere near as much help as what *you* are willing to face up to. I can do nothing with lies, evasions or half-truths. But I can always come close to someone who is honest. No matter how bad the truth is, telling me the truth is always the first step on the road to freedom.

To answer your subsequent question: yes, of course I am here. But I don't necessarily answer the first time someone calls. I wait for the right moment to speak. When I am silent it is to help them recognise how much they need an answer. Then it stops being a game – and becomes deadly serious.

(By the way, I don't get, as you said, 'busy'. I am full of creativity and life, but also always full of energy.)

Remember, I am here – accessible to those who are truly honest. Finally, you might like to know that almost always when people accuse me of not speaking to them, the problem is that they are not listening. In fact, usually they're shouting so loudly that they cannot hear my whisper. The part of my book that says, 'Be still and know that I am God' has always been one of my favourite bits!

Looking forward to your next.

From your fond Father in deepest heaven,

GOD

Dear . . . Oh, God, it really is you!

OK, look, I'm really really sorry but, yes, as we both know, the choirmistress was not the end of my venality. I spent most of my early teens and twenties bedding anything that moved, with no thought for the consequences. 'Sowing my wild oats', as my dad would say – when he was around, which wasn't often, as you know. I do feel bad about that lovely born-again Canadian girl. She was blonde and lithe and supple and had such a 'need to know'. For a while back there I did think I loved her . . . but what did I know then about love?

And, yes, there was the unfortunate incident in Bayswater with the Arab princess and the carving knife but, honest to God – oops, sorry, so sorry – but I was worried she'd cut off my dangly bits when she got moody and started waving that thing at me. So I legged it.

But my real problem now is this . . .

I got married to a lovely girl called Helen and had my own business selling second-hand cars. Not dodgy stuff, you understand – classic cars like Aston Martin DB3s, a Bentley S3 and a couple of Rollers, the odd sports car. Well, after seven years' marriage I didn't so much have an itch as an infestation and pretty soon I was up to my old habits again. To cut a long story short, I took this woman for a test drive in this gorgeous Aston Martin and we ended up on the hard shoulder with her laughing gear . . . well, let's just say I fell for her, big time.

I mean, it's been ages since Helen and I . . . you know. I think she forgot how to . . .

Anyway, it's like I'm entranced by this Lola (nice name, eh?), so I started having an affair with her, only to find out she's married to Eddie 'Cutter' Fast, one of the biggest villains around. He buys and sells commodities, if you know what I mean. Sugar, coffee, and did I mention cocaine? He has an office in Stratton Street, in Mayfair, and it all looks proper but is just a massive front. And I won't tell you how he got his nickname. But I guess you already know.

So – Lola was coming round to the gaff above my business twice a week for some loving and then last week she drops the bombshell and tells me she thinks Eddie knows about us.

He knows where I live, he knows where my wife and kids live, and I'm just terrified he's going to come for us and hack us to pieces. On top of that, Lola's ardour seems to have cooled a little . . . what can I do? Help me, God. PLEASE.

Billy

Billy, my dear boy,

Your last letter truly saddened me. It was a typical example of confession of the 'nudge, nudge, wink, wink, you know what I mean, squire?' variety.

In almost everything you said you evaded the truth, presenting me with a fictionalised version of what really happened. You skip so lightly across those moments where you devastated people by winning them with your easy charm, using them, and then abandoning them.

What really saddens me in all this is that you fail to see that the person you have most devalued is yourself. Two things have marked you ever since your choirboy days. You always evaded real commitment, most of all commitment to me. You came near enough to be able to scrape acquaintance, but never to enter true relationship. And hand in hand with ducking commitment has gone the avoidance of truth-telling.

You speak with smirking innuendo of the shabby way you broke your marriage vows. When you describe your initial encounter with Lola, just tell it like it is: oral sex is not a shock to me. What wounds me is the sordid defiling of her vows, your own betrayal of your covenant with Helen and the loyalty you owed to your children. You wrap your encounters in a phoney glamour because you do not want to look directly at what you have done, or what you have become.

You see, underneath the bravado there is shame – and I did not make you to live in shame. I want you to be free of it, and free from fear too. Even as you are reading this letter I hear you thinking, 'Yes, but what about Eddie Fast and his well-earned reputation for cutting those who mess with him?' Something like this was always going to happen. Thousands of years ago, Moses told my ancient people, 'Be sure your sins will track you down.' Do you see that, Billy? The chaos you have sown is rising up and gathering speed like a cruise missile programmed to seek you out and destroy you.

The Arab princess has become just a funny story for you, a laugh with your mates: 'Aren't I Jack the lad?' Her father and her brother were very angry. You defiled their family honour – she could have died. Because you cried out to me in fear, I hid you from them.

Then there's Sara. I allowed her to come into your life to raise you up, not to be dragged down by you. She was devastated.

And what about your wife, Helen, with your two little boys and girl? She had a lot on her plate, but you put all the responsibility for Lola on her. Do you really think you are the only man whose marriage has become flat and a little boring? Your wife 'wasn't interested'? Did you ever stop to ask why on earth she should be interested in a man who was so profoundly uninterested in her as a person? Her deepest wounds are not from the act of betrayal so much as the fact that you stopped seeing her as a person at all.

Now: are you beginning to understand why I found your last letter so painful to read?

It is quite simple – I am your real Dad, and I love you more than you can ever know. I believe in you and I am proud of you, proud of the real William that is still there inside the impressive-looking façade. The real you, the real William, was created to be a conqueror, like his namesake, winning over all the wretched circumstances of your life.

Yes, your father was appalling, and his father was even more appalling to him. But you are not a robot. Your response to what happened to you has always in the end been your own responsibility. So, stop using him as an excuse. I am not proud of the 'whining' Billy you've shown me so far: I made you to be different from that.

So come on, son, it is time for you to face up and be the man I dreamed of in eternity before the world even existed.

Your loving Father,

GOD

You tosser! What do you know about anything? You didn't have to hide under the stairs with your sister on the odd occasions your dad actually came home for fear he'd drag one or both of us off to abuse us. 'Come here, you! And you . . . you can watch! Just do as you're told!'

Your mum didn't get cancer when you were four, either. What do you know about pain? And in any event, if you're everything you're cracked up to be, why did you stand on the sidelines and do nothing? So I've been a 'naughty boy'. Ha! What do you expect? I was left to find my own way, and the choir was the only really safe place for me, somewhere I could get lost in the music and the way Celia's gown would swish about, and I was just beginning to see the light and then you took my mum away . . .

Ten years she fought that vile disease . . . she knew what was going on, but she was powerless to stop it, wasn't she? She was too ill to do anything. Do you know what it's like to see a person literally fight for life? To watch their every breath regulated by a machine, for strangers to come into your house with frozen faces and sad smiles, for doctors to talk about palliative care and look very grave, for your sister to be continually crying and for you not to be able to stop ANY OF IT!!

And then one day the machine is switched off and the person you loved most in the world is gone. Just lying there. A bag of bones.

So, yes, maybe I've been a bad boy, but what the hell did you expect? A saint? And you? You just watched. YOU COULD HAVE STOPPED IT!

Billy

Dear Billy,

So, 'no more mister nice guy!' eh? We *are* making progress.

You ask what I know about suffering. That is because you persist in the belief that I live in some remote location called heaven where angels sit on clouds, plinking away on golden harps as saints of the past waft by. Eternal sunshine beams out of everlasting blue skies, while disembodied spirits bring cups of ambrosial delight, and occasionally from this privileged and far-off celestial vantage point I put the telescope to my eye to see what is happening on Planet Earth. It is a common misconception.

Understand this: I am not an absent creator, still less a 'Blind Watchmaker'.

I am *the* Creator and everything I make is filled with who I am. Nothing happens in all creation I am not instantly aware of. I am present in every part. Not a molecule, not an atom, not even a single subatomic particle exists without being filled with my beauty and glory.

So, think about it – I was present in every particle of your body, and of your sister's body, when your father was abusing you. I felt all your pain, and I feel it still. Even more appalling, I was present in every molecule of your father's body as he abused you. I was there in the inner synapses of his brain as the pain of childhood memories drove him to repeat the pattern. I was pleading with him to let me heal him – but he ran from me.

Do you understand what I am saying? Your pain and your suffering are present with me now. I still hear the screams of the millions who died in the Holocaust. I hear their cries of reproach, 'God, where are you?' I am torn apart by the twisting of my glorious vision for humanity in the guards who slaughtered them, the millions betrayed and murdered by the very leaders they put their trust in.

What about you? Do you hear the cry of every woman raped and defiled? Or the mothers desperately trying to feed their children at breasts shrivelled by starvation? Or the lost childhood of tens of thousands of children, some as young as eighteen months, in the sex shops of Bangkok?

You think you are angry? Your anger is insignificant compared to the holy anger building inside me. Judgement must come, one day.

So, my dear Billy, understand this: I know pain. I live it every day.

I am truly sorry for your pain. Selfish anger and unforgiveness are uncomfortable bedfellows. But there is a way forward. I will be in touch soon.

Your Father,

GOD

God – it's me again. I just don't understand. I don't get it when you say, 'I am there.' What do you mean?

By the way, sorry for calling you a tosser.

Billy

Dear Billy,

Thank you for your note.

Let me try and explain a little more. I am God over all creation. Every family on earth gets its true name from me. When I see my children abused and defiled it breaks me, too . . .

For tens of thousands of years of human history I have heard the cries of the oppressed, the unjustly imprisoned, – all their pain, all their suffering – and the twisting of the humanity of those who inflicted it. I carry within me the terrible litany of human cruelty and pain. To you, the pain of those long gone, the pain of the dead, is remote, historical. To me, Billy, it is ever-present.

Eternity is my dwelling-place. I touch every single moment of history, from the beginning to the end. I see it all even now. Those long dead are not long gone to me. They are as alive as you are; their pain as present and real; their cruelties and agonies, guilt and despair are all within me, always present.

To you, all this pain would seem not only unbearable but unending. But it does have limits. As there was a beginning, so there will be an end of time and all its pain. That is what my Son did on the cross. He carried your pain – all of it! Every cry of agony from your sister and the tortured torment of your father's darkened soul – he carried it all. Do you think he went through all that just so respectable people could go to church on a Sunday morning and sing mournfully, 'Make thy chosen people joyful'?

The physical torment of his death, painful as it was, gripping as it is to your artists and film-makers, was nothing compared to what we endured together as I, his father downloaded into him the vileness and pain, the guilt and despair of broken humanity. He chose to bear that weight. I was and am so proud of him.

So I know about your pain, Billy, about the loss of your mum. And you were wrong about her – she was not too ill to do anything. She prayed constantly for you. You were the cry of her heart from the moment you were born until her last breath. She loved your sister, of course, but she saw the danger of the seeds of rage deep inside you. Why do you think you found the choir such a refuge? I made you and I know you. Music has always been the language of your heart.

Do I know what it's like to see someone fight for their life? Yes. I know what that's like – and not just in the privileged surroundings of your Western hospitals. I see the same struggle where the unwashed poor die in the gutters.

Their children also cry out for it to stop.

You asked why I stood on the sidelines and did nothing. You say, 'YOU COULD HAVE STOPPED IT!' Yes, I could. But my justice is not selective. I don't play favourites. If I stop one man in his tracks then I have to stop all human beings. For it to be truthful, judgement must be fair, it must be universal. You want me to stop it – where can I start? With you?

You seduced and abandoned Sara – do you remember Sara? Her family wanted you dead. Her father prayed, 'Lord, if there is any justice, you will kill him.' Why did

I not give in to his request? Because I looked down the years and saw the possibility of redemption. The angry, whining Billy, self-centred, filled with pain and inflicting pain on others, could become a hero, and – yes, indeed – why not a saint!?!

You did ask.

Now the anger has begun to flow out instead of being dammed up inside you by cynicism and a determination not to be vulnerable or hurt ever again. There is a real possibility that you could indeed be what I have always believed you could be. Not Billy the kid, but William the real conqueror – saint, hero and son.

Your ever-loving Dad,

GOD

PS Thanks for the apology – but just so that you know, I don't indulge in pointless self-gratification. My energy is given to pouring out my love on others. I know it's just a conventional insult but I felt I should put the record straight!

Dear God,

Thanks for your letter. You don't pull any punches, do you?

I don't really know what to write ... I'm just so lost and angry. But I know you're already aware of that.

But feeling other people's pain ... bloody hell ... do you really? And if so, how do you cope?

I just don't get it. I know about the forty days and forty nights thing, and the devil tempting you, and how you chose not to rise to his bait, but you're meant to be able to fix things ... I mean, that's what I was always taught. You know, miracles and all that.

I'm still trying to work you out. Maybe you're just like the rest of us, frail as breath and human in every way.

I didn't understand a huge amount of what you wrote, but you're God, so you're bound to be a megabrain ... and me? I'm just Billy Fidget, heartbreaker and heartbroken. I knew I'd hurt Sara by promising her the earth and then stealing away her virtue that night when she'd had a glass of wine too many.

Actually you know, don't you?

About the Rohypnol ... it was tantamount to rape, I guess. She didn't say much at the time – a little cry when I entered her and then just big, silent tears soaking into the pillow. I was fortunate that she didn't go to the police for a few days, otherwise I'd have been banged up for sure. I hate myself for what I did.

What kind of scum takes advantage like that?

I'm such a bad man. What I don't get is this: if you can shine light into every dark corner of my life, then why do you still love me? It doesn't make sense.

Most people I've hurt or taken advantage of just cut me off, walk away or lash out, but you – ?

You're different.

I don't understand anything any more.

Who am I ? What have I become?

And why do you call yourself my ever-loving Dad? The only father I knew was a brilliant inflictor of the most twisted pain you can imagine. Not just physical but emotional and psychological, too. He was deeply evil.

I want to change but I'm too far gone. I'm way past my sell-by date.

I just want Helen and my kids to be safe . . . I don't care about myself any more, but please, please – I'm begging you! Do something, anything to save them, before that bastard Eddie Fast gets his hands on them.

You know if you want me to sell my soul to you, I will.

I'm yours! But please, please, save my family.

You're all I've got.

Billy

Billy, my boy,

You are in a state, aren't you? But it's encouraging. Your anxiety is not just for yourself, but for your wife and children. Feeling for others is an essential step on the road to learning to love. Mind you, I had to laugh when Billy the wheeler-dealer came out to try to sell me his soul! We'll look at that a bit later.

You ask how I cope with feeling the pain and torment of every member of the human race. I endure it because I never stop believing in each one of them.

And I never stop believing because I never stop loving.

My love is always bigger than their guilt or their pain. I concentrate on them as people. I always see their faces.

When you speak about the forty days and nights of temptation in the wilderness, you need to understand that the greatest pain was knowing my Son had to endure that totally alone.

One temptation was the chance to 'fix things', as you put it – to turn stones into bread. He refused, though he could have done it. My Son and I do not believe in short cuts or quick fixes. That's why I look for genuine confession.

Real confession is never about a quick fix. It's about longing for real transformation. So, well done. You admitted that what you did to Sara was one of the lowest points in your life. You're beginning to get it. It's not enough that I know what you did; you have to actually say it to yourself, and to me, if you're going to be free. So it's a good start.

But the Rohypnol – there's the old Billy coming through again – 'tantamount to rape'? I don't think so. It *was* rape! Although she was almost paralysed by the drug, that little cry was heard in heaven as a scream of horror. You had betrayed her trust. Violated her.

But love held her back from going to the police until it was too late for them to prove anything.

What kind of scum takes advantage like that? Your kind of scum, Billy. I see deeper into every dark corner of your life than you can even imagine. So how can I love you when I know all that's going on?

It's simple – I love you for who you are, though I hate with a passion things you do. That's why I have never given up on you.

But the worst thing was not the sexual violation. You took what you wanted from Sara. Then you abandoned her in a city where she knew no one. She tried to kill herself. When her father prayed that I would kill you, he was sitting by her hospital bed watching his daughter dying, pleading for her life. He is a good man. But he discovered hatred that day. He hated what you had done and hated you.

It almost overwhelmed him. He raged at me, demanding revenge. But then he remembered hearing the saying 'The best revenge is to win the offender', and he determined to take vengeance on the powers that drove you by winning you to me. He came to a place of peace, yielding his daughter to me. My Spirit gave his voice power, and his prayers drew her back from the gates of death.

Determined to seek a better revenge, he began to pray for you. Every day he went to war on your behalf. He became your true father. His prayers formed a slender but unbreakable cord of grace from you to me.

So, what are you at this moment? What have you become? You've become what you most hate – a repeat of your dad: weak, selfish and pathetic, a bully taking advantage of others too weak to retaliate, an abuser of children.

When you met Sara she was innocent and trusting, like a child. When you took her and violated her, you truly became your father's son.

It is often the way. People become what they hate.

But it's not all bad news. You're not too far gone. It's not true that you are beyond redemption. Past your sell-by date? I don't think so. But writing yourself off is the easy way out. It saves you from facing up to the painful work of confession and repentance. I know you can become what I designed you to be. Sara's father believes it. He got that faith from me. As I said before, I've always believed in you.

Your always-loving Father in deepest heaven,

GOD

God,

I still don't get it. How can you know all I do, and say, 'I still believe in you?'

What you said about hate – I have hated my dad every day of my life. And you're right, I have become him. Why should you care about me? I disgust myself. I offered to sell you my soul. Why would you want it?

Billy

22

Billy, my dear son,

The answer to your question is simple.

I love you.

When you offered to sell me your soul, you were confusing me with someone else. I am a father, not a trader. The enemy of men's souls is a trader and would cheerfully accept your soul at any price in order to drag it into hell with himself. Misery loves company!

But I have never wanted to own you. I want you to be my son and let me be the father you never had. Deep inside of you there is a secret part – your spirit – which was made for union with me. But without your permission I cannot ever enter that place. It would be a total violation. I am waiting for you to open the door freely, happily, like a kid. I know you are a wheeler-dealer, but there can be no trading here. If you give yourself to me I will give myself to you. It is a relationship.

So, I don't want to buy your soul. It's soaked in every vile trick you have ever pulled, every lying word you've ever spoken, every betrayal of everybody you ever conned. As it is, it stinks to high heaven – literally! Remember that job lot of luxury cars you got from your gangster pal? The Lamborghini had had a dead body in the boot. You never could get rid of the smell. Or the day your dog rolled in the rotting fish by the lake? You got him home and he stank the house out. You scrubbed him. You chased him round the house, spraying him with deodorant. The kids joined in with perfumes of all kinds. But nothing stopped the smell!

Just like that, your soul needs something more radical than expensive fragrance.

You ask me to keep Helen and the kids safe. I will. I will save them from Eddie Fast.

But can I save them from you? People don't just inherit money, houses, cars; they inherit the spiritual toxicity or health of their parents. You received a poisonous inheritance from your father. You have been walking in it ever since. And you're passing it on to them.

Would you really do anything to save your children? Truly? Come clean. You said, 'You're all I've got.' That is true. I am all you've got. But people amaze me with their ability to ignore reality and flee relationship, ducking away at the last minute.

So will you dare to stop running, turn around and begin to walk towards me? It will take courage to walk into the arms of a dad. Can you trust that I will not abuse you but will accept and heal you; not defile you but cleanse you? It's time. Now!

Will you give yourself to me, holding nothing back? Promise to walk in the truth? If you will then at last we can start – you can begin the adventure.

Your ever-loving Dad,

GOD

PS If you really want to know, ownership of your soul was claimed by the enemy. But I have already bought it back so that I can set you free. Some things are priceless.

Dear God,

I don't know what to say to your last letter. I am so sorry for all the crap. You know I tried going into a church the other day, but the people weren't exactly welcoming – kind of all smiles but remote, if you know what I mean. It didn't feel real, like a house with no upstairs, and no one wants to live in one of those, do they?

So I did try. Honest. I'm tired of my life and the way I've been living – always on the edge, just one step ahead of trouble.

And I want to put things right. But how can I undo all the evil I've done? When I think of Sara I feel sick at what I did. I have a daughter now and I'd kill anybody who did that to her.

And all the women – yes, I just took them. Most were willing but it . . . they . . . meant nothing to me – just somewhere to park my car and let go. Fairly instant self-gratification. No thought for them. Just me. Always selfish, pathetic me, wreaking revenge on my mother and womankind for all she allowed – and you know she knew – and for all the pain caused by her looking the other way. And there I am perpetuating the cycle of lust and hatred, breaking Helen's patient heart in the process.

Bitter and broken.

And you are God, I know that now . . . so thank you for keeping my family safe.

I'm at a loss for what to say about that. Words fail me. Just like I fail myself. But I think I've found a way out of this mess, God. I'm convinced the world will be a better place without me. So this is the last letter you're going to get. I've got enough booze and sleeping pills to see me comfortably numb and into the arms of whatever lies ahead of me. Just one big fat joint to take the edge off before I go.

I just hope you're not lying and that you'll be there. Goodbye.

Billy

Billy, my dear son,

Well, that definitely wasn't the smartest move of your life, was it? How did you enjoy A&E? Not much fun? Do you remember the stomach pump? Probably not very well. Those who are conscious find it rather unpleasant. The self-harm team took very good care of you. It was the paramedic who found you on your garage forecourt; you were lucky one of the firemen didn't tread on you.

I suppose an explanation would be helpful, since you weren't conscious for much of what happened. The last puff on your spliff sent you into oblivion. You dropped the joint, it rolled into a corner of the sofa and you slumped on to the floor, dead to the world – as they say.

Your actions posed a tricky dilemma to the special agent who has responsibility for watching over you (in popular culture these agents are commonly called angels). Instructions given to all these guardians are that they are to respect the decisions of the humans they watch over. But you and I were in the middle of a conversation. You have not yet responded to the question I posed at the end of my last letter.

Do you see what I mean about people ducking away at the last minute? Some people will do anything to avoid a difficult decision. But setting fire to your apartment is by anybody's standards more than a little extreme!

In addition, I promised that I would save your family. Like many men, you mistakenly think of your family as something that is separate from you. But you, Billy, are central to it. You are the father, you are Dad. Your culture is going through a period of madness where it pretends that fathers are incidental adjuncts to family life. But your role as loving husband and loyal dad is pivotal to them all.

So the agent who watches over you was given permission to take human form. He scooped you up from the floor of the smoke-filled room just as the sofa burst into flames. You suffered some minor burns which will be painful but not truly serious. They will serve as a reminder that actions have consequences.

Don't forget it.

Please do not do anything as stupid as this again. Yes, I want you in my eternal home – but not sneaking in too early through the back door, shame-faced and alone. I dream that when your time comes you will enter through the main gates, flung wide open, with millions of angels cheering the homecoming of a winner of life's marathon.

You have a long race to run before you get that crown.

You said you were convinced the world would be a better place without you. Convinced by whom? Your own thoughts are not very reliable, and the one who whispers such ideas only wants to suck you into a dark, downward spiral that leads to depression and death. Don't listen!

Remember I believe in you. My love *never* gives up.

And don't forget that I'm the one who decides when the world will be better off without somebody. That is not your prerogative.

Be encouraged: it is good to have you understand at last what all your affairs were really about. They almost never had anything to do with love. You were taking revenge, as you rightly said, wreaking havoc in their lives just as your mother and father wreaked havoc in yours. Realising this is real progress.

You mentioned Helen's heart is broken. Bitter and broken. You realise what that means? It means she truly loves you. Do you remember that bit of my book 'He has sent me to bind up the broken-hearted'?

I know you remember. It made an impact on you when you were a choirboy, because you knew the dull, lonely ache of a broken heart.

I sent my Son to heal. That has been our intention from the very beginning. I am sending you back to do what you have never done before: to work with patience, kindness and thankful love to mend Helen's broken heart. To remove from her the poisoned barbs of rejection and bitterness.

As for undoing all the evil you've done and putting everything right – let me take that burden from you. Only I can do that, and I will.

Just trust me.

Do what you can to put things right. Write letters of apology; tell Sara's dad that you want to accept my offer of relationship. Because you do, don't you? That was why you decided you would go to a church. I know the one you mean. I've been trying to get into that place myself for years!

But it was the wrong way round. Inside the church or outside, I am close to those whose minds and hearts are towards me. Those who turn to me find I run to meet them. In the end the decision remains in your hands.

So, here I am, your Father, waiting: waiting for you to come home, waiting for you to say yes to the question I asked you at the end of my last letter. In case you have forgotten, here it is again –

Will you dare to turn around and walk towards me? Take courage and walk into the arms of a dad? Will you trust that I will love you, not abuse you; accept and heal you; not defile you but cleanse you?

It really is time – right now.

So will you give yourself to me? Holding nothing back? Walk in the truth? If you will dare to, then at last we can start – you can begin the adventure.

Will you embark upon the dream, the destiny I crafted for you in eternity?

It still waits. And I wait.

Your ever-loving Dad,

GOD

PS I have never lied, nor will I ever.

Dear God,

The answer is yes, but . . . I have to see you.
When can we meet?

Love,

Billy

Billy!

Nice move!

I have to hand it to you – that was a very fancy piece of footwork. Neat avoidance, done so slickly; it hardly looks like what it is. A wonderful economy with words.

It really illustrates what I said to you. Nothing amazes me so much as the capacity of human beings to slip away from relationship at the last minute.

Let's start with your answer, 'yes, but . . .' What I am looking for is for you to have the courage to simply say yes without any buts, ands or maybes.

Just a simple YES is what I am looking for.

And here is my question for you: what do you mean by 'see me'? What have you ever truly seen in your life that is of real importance to you? Have you, for instance, ever seen Helen? I believe you have, but not with your eyes. Oh yes, she is a beautiful woman to look at, and in spite of bearing you three children she still has a good figure. But you have known and had plenty of women who looked good and had great figures.

You told me they were just a place to park your car. In other words, you never truly saw them. Yet when you think of Helen, you don't just think of a gorgeous-looking woman, you think of loyalty, love, sacrifice, pain, compassion. You *see* her. You are beginning to see the things that really matter.

So you have already begun to see me.

Do you know what's involved in sight?

Light is reflected or refracted from or through an object, and light in its various wavelengths is then received in your eye. The lens of your eye is bent in order to give a sharp and accurate image on the retina.

If you are going to see anything clearly you have to focus. That applies to seeing me. The physical process illustrates the spiritual one. Get the focus right and you will begin to see me everywhere.

You have seen something of me in creation. On those rare occasions when you took the time to look at the beauty of a sunset, a storm on a mountain, a raging sea or a quiet river, you began to sense the wonder growing inside you – awe – and in a panic you quickly backed away. You have also seen me in the love that Helen has shown you, and in the eyes of your children you have sensed something of my heart – that moment when your heart lurches as your daughter runs towards you, shouting 'Daddy, Daddy!'

You have already seen me, Billy. I am there in the world I made. In the relationships that matter. In the beauty of the music you love, that moves you to tears. I'm there in the best stories, in the films that make you feel as though you too could be a hero.

But if you want to see me in clearest focus, read the story. Look into the book that unveils my deep and abiding love affair with humanity. Focus on my Son. In him I have most clearly unveiled myself. He is the fulfilment of all the promises I made to my ancient people. You already have a contemporary version of my book. Start there. Begin with one of the portraits of my Son. And begin with a prayer: ask me to show you Jesus as I see him for you today.

My Holy Spirit will answer that prayer more quickly than you would believe.

By the way, I am not saying you will never see me with your physical eyes. That may happen in this life. But you will need to be prepared for it. If I were to unveil myself to you now as I truly am, I would destroy you. The blazing power of my love would burn you. The clear light of my truth would cut like a laser beam, and the utter unworldliness of my eternal, heavenly reality would completely unmake your frail physical body.

But Billy, here is the promise – if you really mean it when you say yes, and I believe you do, one day you *will* see me. By then you will be fully equipped, not just to see me in all my glory, but to receive my glory. On that day, you yourself will be amazing.

You ask when we can meet. NOW! All you have to do is stop running, stop ducking and diving, stop avoiding that which you most fear – me. By now you know that I love you and that my love is unconditional. You know I'm not going to punish you for all your many misdeeds. I am going to forgive you. That is what most frightens you. You fear above all the love that will peel away your defences, touch the places where you have been so deeply wounded, and cleanse the defilement of your years.

So we can meet right now. If you will just say yes. Say yes to my great Son. You always wanted a big brother and he is the biggest of them all. Imagine all he has endured for you. All the horrible, vile, terrible things done to you by your father passed through his body, his mind, his soul. He knows, and because he knows, I know. And all the nasty tricks you ever pulled, all the people you used, misused and abused, all passed through him. He carried the lot for you, Billy – my Son, your big brother. Say yes to him, let his Spirit join with your spirit and you become my son for ever.

It will be so good to welcome you into the family.

From your loving Father in deepest heaven,

GOD

Dear Mr Frederiksen,

I'm sorry that I don't know your full name. This is going to be a hard letter to receive – it's hard enough to write – but my name is William Fidget (better known to you as Billy) and back in the nineties I dated your daughter Sara while she was over here on her gap year. She loved me, and I loved her, but she would never give into my desire to 'go the whole way'. Well, I'm very sorry to say I am the vile creature that spiked her drink and robbed her virtue. I understand that as a result of my actions she became acutely depressed and tried to take her own life.

Now I don't blame you for hating me or wanting me dead for what I did, but I feel like I don't have much time left and I want to put things right.

I am so sorry. That sounds rubbish, doesn't it, after all the terrible pain my actions have caused you and your family. But I am truly sorry and I am prepared to do ANYTHING to try and put it right . . . and I know that sounds trite because I can't undo what I've done, but I just wanted you to know that the shame and the sorrow, the guilt and the grief hang round me like a cloud of toxic fog.

You see, I'm learning to breathe for the first time in my life. I'm trying to get close to God (seems like I tried everything else and nothing seems to work), so I'm sorry. I hope you understand why I'm trying to get in touch . . . I just wanted to say I'm SO VERY SORRY.

Please write back. Something. Anything.

Yours truly,

William A. Fidget

Mr Fidget,

I opened your letter addressed to Mr Frederiksen at this address. You sure have a nerve writing to us. I imagine from its content that its intended recipient was my father.

I am Sara's brother. What you did to Sara is well known in our family, and I am not of a mind to offer you any forgiveness whatsoever. What happened to Sara was appalling. My father's misguided desire to forgive you caused estrangement between the two of us. We did not speak for many years, but have recently been in contact again.

After his retirement he moved to a house near the coast. I do not intend to give you his address.

For my part, I would happily tear up your letter and pretend it never arrived. However, there is always a risk that you will manage to contact him, and if he were to discover I had done that, it would only result in further estrangement. I will therefore forward your letter to him. Whether he replies to you or not is entirely his choice. If he chooses not to do so, please do not send any further communications to this address. I have no desire to make acquaintance with a person who has done so much damage not only to my sister but to my whole family. In my opinion, my father should make no response to your letter. But he is, as I have already indicated, irrationally committed to this notion of forgiveness.

It is not one that I share.

I will forward a copy of my response in the hope that it may encourage him to take the right course of action and have nothing whatever to do with you.

Yours,

Thor Frederiksen

God? What the hell are you doing?! How could you do that to me? Why did you let my letter fall into the wrong hands when you knew I was trying to apologise? Now I've got yet another person on the planet who hates my guts and would rather I was dead. I'll never be able to put things right! You could have made it easier for me, and yet you didn't. I don't get it! I'm trying to do the decent thing here and you allow things to get worse.

Now just where's the love in that?

You disgust me!

Billy

Billy,

Good to hear from you – at last!

The answer to your first question is I am doing what I know to be best. Best for you, for Sara and her father, for Thor. And of course what's best for Helen and the children.

How could I do it to you? With sorrow – for the pain I knew it would cause you – yet with great love. You see, my aim is not to make you comfortable. I dream of you becoming the hero that deep down you long to be. My task is to have you pass through things you don't want to face, so that you may become all you dream of being.

Yes, I knew you were trying to apologise. I also knew that, even more than Mr Frederiksen senior, Thor Frederiksen needed to see the letter you wrote. He has been held a prisoner of the past for too long. Your letter is going to have a massive impact on his life, like the fall of the first stone that triggers an avalanche. I work with long-term plans – for your good and your ultimate joy.

Think about it – Sara's brother hates you because of what you did years ago. He has hated you ever since. Your letter didn't cause his hatred. It exposed it. The only thing that's changed is now you know that he hates you. You also know more about the impact of what you did than before. You're speaking the truth when you say you will never be able to put things right – at least, not on your own.

But if you and I walk together you will be amazed at what can happen. Yes, I could have made it easier for you. But in the end, that would have made matters worse. I told you long ago that I love you, my son, and I do. And yes, from your perspective I allowed things to get worse. You must try to understand: I never act from any motive besides love. I allowed your letter to fall into the 'wrong' hands – because I love every person who has played a part in this sad story.

When I let you try to work things out without drawing on my wisdom or strength, that's when you find out you've only made things worse. I am not acting in mere sentimentality but in love – burning love of a passion and purity you could not even begin to imagine. It drives me to action and holds me in moments of restraint. I hold back because I am waiting for you to turn to me at last.

Do you get it? I am still waiting for the answer to my question. Will you finally surrender yourself to my Son and enter into the Father–son relationship with me for which you were created?

Like so many, you mistakenly think that before you can give yourself to me you must straighten things out. If you are to enter the freedom I have for you, you have to discover your limitations. It is only when you realise you *can't* that you receive the power that will enable you to find out you *can*. It's simple, really. But it's the hardest thing humans ever have to do. You come to me with empty hands; I fill them with my joy and strength.

So what about it? Are you going to say yes?
Remember – my dreams are always bigger.
Your loving Dad,

GOD

Dear Thor,

I can understand your anger. I have a daughter and I would just hate it if anything so low and dirty as what I did to your sister were to ever happen to her. I know I can't wave a magic wand and make it all right. I wish I could. I live with my past and the execrable waste that was once my life on a daily basis. And I don't want to any more.

So I am sorry.

If you want to . . . then come and find me. I will not hide. Come and do what you want. I am waiting and hoping that you will exact the kind of revenge meted out to people who perpetrate such vile acts.

But before you do, please make good on your promise to deliver the letter to your father. I want him to at least know that I made some kind of effort to ask for his forgiveness. I think he would want that.

Yours truly,

William A. Fidget

Mr Fidget,

I had no intention of being involved in any further correspondence with you, but I find myself forced to answer your latest letter.

I am not the kind of person who indulges in personal vengeance. I will not therefore be coming to find you in order to exact the kind of revenge you mention. I know you would find that satisfying, but I have no wish to help you. You will have to find your peace some other way.

With regard to your asking me to keep my promise to deliver your letter to my father: please note that, unlike some people, I'm a man of honour. When I make a promise, I keep it. Your first letter has already been sent to my father. I am sure he will deal with it as he thinks best.

Yours,

Thor Frederiksen

From: William.a.Fidget@mac.com
Date: 1 June 2009 12:21:39 BDT
To: God@Godinheaven.com
Subject: YES!

Dear God

Yes.

Yes, I will.

I'm so tired of being Billy. I'm desperate to be the man you write about.

Like William the real conqueror.

A hero and not a lowlife.

I'm so completely exhausted with my squalid tawdry existence, so God, Jesus, whoever you are, I want you. I need you.

Please, PLEASE come into my life.

Love,

William

Billy, my dear son,

It was wonderful to receive your letter – to see you write 'yes' at last! Of course, I didn't need to see it written. The moment when finally, deep inside, you said that simple word 'yes', it reverberated from highest to deepest heaven and set all the angels dancing. Though they have never been redeemed, they love to sing the song of the forgiven; they love to celebrate when another son comes home to his Father.

I see you are still confused about the precise way my Son and I relate to each other and to you. From the moment that 'yes' echoed in you, you were incorporated into my eternal son – the mighty Word of God, the one who expresses everything I am, everything I think and do. Through him I made the entire universe. Through him I redeemed the muddied and confused billions of the fallen earth. You became part of him when you said yes to me.

In previous letters I called you son because your unique blend of traits, strengths and talents came straight from me as the Father of all things. In calling you son, I was reminding you of your origin. But now I call you son to remind you of your destiny. Then I called you son because, as one created by me, you were in a general sense my child. But now you are my son by choice. When you said yes, you moved from the general to the specific position of sonship. As you took your place in the Body of my great son, Jesus, you became an inheritor of those promises and titles that I have given to him. Exploring all those is your eternal adventure.

And now that you've decided to say yes, you must stand before the world to say: this is the beginning of a new life, I am turning my back on the old Billy, Billy the kid, Billy liar and I am becoming Billy, son of the best Dad in the universe.

This really is a new start. You become an inheritor of the same words that I spoke to Jesus:

'You are my Son, chosen and marked by my love. I am so proud of you.'

Your loving Dad,

GOD

PS I saw you when you sat on the edge of your bed, bowed your head and finally gave in. Even as you said yes to me, you know something heavy, dark and deadly lifted off you and you felt a new sense of freedom. The warmth that flowed through you from the crown of your head to the soles of your feet was not your imagination. The enemy will tell you it was psychological, that you made it up. Remember, my son, he is a liar, and he has been from the beginning. It is all he has. Take no notice – that warm glow is my loving approval. It is yours from this moment on to eternity.

Dear William,

I finally received your letter, with great rejoicing. My son forwarded it to me, and the postal service did the rest! It took a while to arrive. In the meantime, I understand you wrote to my son again, inviting him to take revenge on you. You have no idea. He has talked for years about killing you. When your first letter arrived, he was enraged. But your second letter caused him to do something he very rarely does. He picked up the phone and called me. Perhaps I should explain . . .

Sara was born two months premature. For months we focused on her. She gained strength and became a bubbly, bouncing toddler, the joy of her mother.

When Sara was eighteen months old, Ingrid, my wife, became pregnant again. We were delighted. But at seven months it all went horribly wrong. She started bleeding – I rushed her into the car to take her to hospital. The baby was born in the car. Ingrid's bleeding became catastrophic. They both died before we reached the hospital. Utterly devastated, I decided there was no God – not for me. How could there be?

Thor was three and a half. He lost his mother, and he lost me, in a single day. I say he lost me because I became obsessed with Sara. She was hauntingly like her mother. I was so determined that she would not only survive but thrive that I neglected my only son.

When Sara was six, she began school. As Thor passed ten, I suddenly realised he was a stranger to me. He had withdrawn into himself and the onset of adolescence simply made it worse. I tried so hard to regain him but it felt as if I had lost him for good.

Then when Sara decided she wanted to go to England to do

47

a year of study, he came round and stayed for a few days. He helped her pack and said goodbye and he and I seemed to be reconciled.

You came on the scene. For a few weeks, Sara's letters were full of happiness, full of wonder at this amazing man, Billy. Then two weeks of silence. I kept calling her apartment but she never answered the phone. At last I got a call from a ward sister in a London hospital. She told me Sara was on the brink of death – she had tried to commit suicide.

As you can imagine, I was completely distraught. I did my best to keep Thor in the picture but he withdrew completely, and I had to fly to England. When I finally brought Sara home, he blamed me for allowing her to go to London, and obviously for all that happened.

For years he refused to speak to me. But he would talk to Sara. He became more and more isolated, more and more angry and bitter.

When your letter came it triggered a crisis. The letter he wrote you was a tiny expression of the hatred he felt, maybe still feels. But your second letter did something strange. Something I could never have foreseen.

He phoned me at 3.00 a.m. I think he had been drinking – a lot! He was almost incoherent at first.

This is what he said to me.

'I wanted to kill him, I wanted to kill him, Dad. I wanted so much to do it. Then I realised I couldn't do it. I despised myself for not being able to take revenge for my beautiful sister. When the first letter came, I went out the back yard, got my gun and shot all kinds of hell out of everything. Then I wrote back and got drunk. When I got the second letter, I realised what a pathetic waster

this man has been. What a mess his life is. I couldn't believe it, I started to feel sorry for him, of all things! Damn him. Damn him to hell. Damn! Damn! Damn!'

He slammed the phone down. When I tried to call back he wouldn't answer. Perhaps now you will understand why he responded the way he did.

As for me, yes, I wanted to kill you. But perhaps you know how difficult God can be. In desperation I turned to him. He would not let me nurture hate in my heart. As I sat beside Sara's bed and pleaded for her life, he kept showing you to me. I was not gracious. 'Screw him! Damn him to hell!' was my response. The only answer was one word – 'Really?' – and then, a few moments later, 'You truly want that on your conscience?'

'Why shouldn't I?' I shouted back. But then I saw a picture of a little kid streaked with dirt and tears, ill-fitting clothes, covered in dust, hiding in a cupboard. I had no idea whether I was truly seeing you or whether it was just my imagination. All I know is that at that moment I began to feel something for this desperate, unloved child who was hiding. I didn't want to forgive but I made up my mind to do it, to agree with God whose grace has always been so good to me – even when I hated him.

So I said, 'Yes, I will forgive. I will pray for that boy.' And I have prayed for that boy ever since. Believe it or not, William, I have learnt to love you and believe in you, and recently, as I was praying for you, I felt something of a huge dark burden lifting from me.

I hope it means something good has happened to you, that you have begun to feel the cloud of toxic fog about which you wrote – the shame, sorrow, guilt and grief – lifting from you. I hope you are beginning at last to breathe God's fresh air.

Thank you for writing. I forgave you years ago and I forgive you now. Sara, by the way, is well and happy. At the moment I don't plan to tell her that I have heard from you. When the time feels right, I will let her know.

Chase the dream, Billy, chase the dream. Don't let anything hold you back. God has got better things for you.

Yours in the love of Christ,

Haakon Frederiksen

Oh God, oh God, oh God! I love you! I've never said that before to anyone – not properly. It's the first time I've ever meant it!

Thank you so much.

For my life . . .

. . . and for loving me.

God, I wrote to Haakon, and his response was just so full of love I almost couldn't believe it. What a man! I can't believe how different everything feels.

Thank you so much for NEVER giving up on me . . . I know I've still got mountains to climb in so many areas of my life, particularly with Helen and the children but, God, I promise that with your help, I'll do it.

I'm living for you now, Jesus, God, Daddy, you! And I love it!

THANK YOU.

Love,

William

Dear Haakon,

Thank you for your letter. I was so humbled by your response – so full of love and forgiveness, yet so real.

So much has been happening to me that I can't quite take it all in. I've got amazing news for you – I've become a child of God! The dirty little boy with the dark burden from underneath the stairs feels like he's been scrubbed all over and made new. I feel different; lighter, for the most part – as if a heavy suit of chain mail has been taken off my back. You may remember that hymn,

> My chains fell off, my heart was free,
> I rose, went forth, and followed Thee.

I used to sing it in the choir as a kid. Well, that's exactly how I feel. I used to work with a bloke who drove me nuts by going on about being saved. I thought he was talking about goalkeeping! But now I understand.

God has been faithful and answered your prayers by saving me – me, of all people! How can that be? I can't get my head round it, but my whole outlook has changed. Even when I look at women now, I see them differently. They're no longer objects to be ogled and taken advantage of if at all possible. If anything they appear more beautiful – but also kind of unreachable. I don't really want or need to chase them around any more. I guess I just want my wife back, and my children too, but I think I've probably got a lot of hard work to do there.

Haakon, I will chase the dream, but I have a few stark realities to deal with first and a lot of making up to do. Thank you for your forgiveness and prayers. I don't really know what else to say . . . but through your ability to forgive and carry on loving and praying, my life has been turned around. All I can do is marvel at that.

If it's ever appropriate, do please tell Sara I am truly sorry.

Yours truly,

William A. Fidget

PS Do also say thanks to Thor for not murdering me (once he's calmed down a bit).

Dear William,

I cannot tell you how glad I was to receive your letter.

Truthfully, I doubted that it would ever happen. The challenge from God to pray for you was the most demanding hurdle I have ever faced. At first it was a road on which every step was painful. I knew that God wanted me to pray for you, but every word felt like a betrayal of Sara. Yet I knew it was paving the way for God's blessing to come to her. Each day I faced the battle to forgive. It was a painful struggle. But now I can see that every agonising step was worth it – just to receive your last letter.

I am thrilled to know your attitudes have changed so much. However, remember this – there really is a devil. Oh, forget the horns and the tail. The real one is far cleverer than that. Jesus calls him the enemy of men's souls – and he is. He hates us, not so much for ourselves, but because he hates God. Every fibre of his being resonates with envy, hatred and rage against God.

When you stepped over the line to become a part of God's family, believe it or not, you became a soldier in heaven's army. Now the devil will turn his attention on you. He may do it subtly. He may do it in a way that is so obviously evil that it will take your breath away.

But he will oppose you.

Here is my advice – don't give in to him. Be aware of his tricks and don't give in. Ask your new heavenly Father to give you wisdom to know how to recognise the subtle attacks and how to stand up under the sudden shock of an outright assault upon you or your family.

Remember this, dear son – because I think of you as my son in God – Jesus described the devil as 'a liar and the father of lies'.

He is so twisted that even when he speaks the truth he turns it into a lie. Therefore, when he represents himself to you as God's equal or even as more powerful than God, remember he is a liar. Do not fall for his tricks. Remember that whatever he throws at you, God is always bigger.

Oh, and the other thing to remember is this – no matter how powerful he may appear to be right now, he will lose in the end.

Thank you again for writing. It has filled me with a fierce and wonderful sense of victory. God is great!

Regarding Sara, when it is appropriate I will tell her about what God has done in you. As for Thor, he is facing his own struggles. Perhaps you could pray for him – he needs all the help he can get!

Your friend in God,

Haakon Frederiksen

William, my son,

You have no idea how much joy fills heaven when a young member of the family says, with all his or her heart, 'I love you, God.' That single phrase enters eternity and becomes entwined with the angels as they weave their way in and out of the great dance, creating increasingly intricate and beautiful designs. It is gloriously true, as one of your prophets has said, that 'Joy is the serious business of heaven.' The laughter of heaven is deep, rhythmic, holy, happy. The enemy simply cannot stand it. Whenever possible let it fill you.

I love you too, my son. I am glad you were pleased with Haakon's response to you. He is a man who has suffered much to learn how to express my heart. You have begun to feel just a little of that yourself. That is why everything feels different. I have put my Spirit in you and that Spirit never gives up. Let him guide you and draw you ever deeper into my heart and purposes.

You do indeed have mountains to climb – some much more difficult than you can currently imagine. But when circumstances threaten you, take a moment to listen to the voice of my Spirit, who says, 'With God, nothing is impossible!'

Your loving Father,

GOD

PS Just as I called you and challenged you to become the true William, so now I release you to become the true Billy: Billy, who is my boy, my little son – small but called to be mighty.

Eddie Fast: Calling from the plush confines of his office in Mayfair

Billy . . . Eddie Fast here. Just wanted you to know there's going to be a bit of a party at your house – or should I say a fry-up . . . Do you still have all the child-proof locks on the windows? Are you insured? . . . Good. Bye.

God – help!
Aarrghh!
No – not my children . . .
Not Helen!
God?! **. . .**

Billy, my son. Don't panic!

Don't be afraid – I say this to my children over and over again. Don't be afraid, no matter what the circumstances may be. I am God: Creator of all things and Commander of the armies of heaven. There is no other like me and I am your true Father. No matter what Eddie Fast may do, he cannot overturn the laws of the universe. You, my son, are chosen and marked by my love. Anyone who touches you touches the apple of my eye and they will receive full payment.

I promised you I'd keep Helen and the children safe. I will do that. This does not mean they will not face threats or pass through danger. My Son never promised that following his path, walking in my kingdom, would be an easy ride. It is not. But it is one in which you will be changed to become all I have dreamed of.

All this was foreseen. The real battle is to be fought in you. Fight to trust me. Refuse to surrender to fear. Give it all to me and in return receive courage – the courage of my great Son Jesus. He will sustain you.

So remember, no matter what happens, TRUST. Trust and don't be afraid. Stand firm in your faith. You have only just begun. You have within you the seeds of greatness – my seed. It is going to be a rough ride, but my purposes will succeed.

No matter how things may appear, you are in my hands, watched over, loved, secure.

Do what is right and wise for the family's protection, and trust.

Your always loving Father in deepest heaven,

GOD

Dear God,

It's all right for you. It's not your wife and kids, is it? Don't panic?! I did panic – massively. I know I've got you on my side, and that you're in control, but I still feel frightened about all that. It's all new, you see.

But you were as good as your word – Helen and the children are all OK. Well, when I say OK, what I mean is, thank God – sorry, thank you – they were out when Eddie's henchmen threw the petrol bomb through the front window. Our furniture was more or less burnt to a cinder. We have very little left, but at least we have each other.

Or we did. I'm enclosing a letter from Helen for you to read.

I don't get it. I finally start to piece my life together, and then this happens.

What's it all about?

Anyway, please read on and let me know what I have to do, because right now I feel like jacking it all in.

William

Enc:

Dear Billy,

This is not an easy letter to write, and it won't be easy for you to read.

The simple truth is I've had enough. I am so tired. The fire was the straw that broke the camel's back. For years I quietly chose to ignore your desperate need to chase anything with a pulse and wearing a skirt. I made excuses, tried to imagine what it must be like to come from a family background like yours. But now I've run out of excuses and, to tell you the truth, the energy to repeat them. I did it because I really loved you. I suppose a part of me always will.

But you put our kids in danger. *That was unforgivable. And I have finally had enough. I'm glad you've gone. I became so sick of you coming home smelling of someone else's perfume, and I've had enough of your lies and evasions, of taking you into my bed and* faking love.

Ironically you are quite good at sex – the mechanics of it. But Billy, if all I wanted was sexual satisfaction, I could have gone online and bought myself a little something. Then I wouldn't have had to fake it. For years now I've been longing for someone to make love to me. But you never understood that. You thought you were good at sex. I suppose you are – in a programmed and technical kind of way. You know the buttons to press. But do you understand how lonely I felt at the very moment of it? To know that you weren't really there, that I was just one of many. All these years I have loved you and longed for you. But I lost you to your constant philandering years ago.

You got drunk and set fire to the apartment above the garage. Now the house has been trashed and the children and I have nowhere to live, and it's all down to you.

You must be so proud!

When I think of how we got into this situation, your selfishness disgusts me. I knew your loving me was a pretence. But I really thought you loved the children. Now I know you didn't even care about them. Maybe you just can't love anybody but yourself.

But now you say you've found God! Well, good for you. I wonder how God will take to you using him the way you use everybody else. The only thing you ever worshipped was yourself and your own selfish desires.

The biggest irony is that underneath I believe there was a decent human being trying to get out. But all you've ever done is crush that. The Billy I love has been killed off, suffocated beneath layers of lies and posturing.

I knew what you were like – but I never thought it would come to this. Now it has.

What hurts most isn't losing the house, it's losing for ever the Billy I once knew and loved. To know that I no longer matter to you the way you matter to me. Even now I remember the way you used to look at me, your eyes burning into mine, and that smile . . . oh God, that smile . . .

I can't believe it – I am crying as I write this.

Well, I bet you've used that smile a thousand times. Was she good, Lola? Was she worth all the aggravation and pain? Did she make you feel big? Did she say, 'Oh yes, Billy – you're the best'?

I bet she did.

You see, we women are not as dumb as you think. We know just how arrogant, insecure and stupid men can be. We massage your vanity.

Well, now she can have you.

Much as I love you, Billy, it's no good: I can't go back, I won't ever go back to that old life. I am at the end of my tether. Putting me at risk is one thing, but putting your boys and your daughter in danger is unforgivable.

So make no mistake – you are to stay away from the children. I'll give you news about them. But you must not come near them. And I won't tell you where we are staying. The kids' safety comes before everything.

Tom is trying to be your replacement. He said to me, 'I'm a big boy now, Mum. I'll take care of you if the bad men come.' Annabel can't understand why she can't see her daddy. All I can tell her is some very nasty men are after her daddy, so Daddy has to stay away to make sure the bad men don't get to us. Little Jack keeps wandering around saying 'Dadda'. As long as you stay away, I'll keep you informed about them. But e-mail is all you're going to get. They're BEAUTIFUL and you've LOST them.

I'm truly sorry. But the fact is, Billy, you brought this on yourself. You should have been their protector. But you put them in danger. When this is all truly over I may be willing to enter negotiations about access. Birthday cards – assuming you remember their birthdays – can be sent to our lawyers.

So we're over. Finished. If you come near me or the kids, God help me I might even save Eddie Fast the job and kill you myself. So just stay away.

Yours,

Helen

Billy, my son, called to be mighty,

Let's start with the end of your letter. Well done! You say you feel like jacking it all in. But instead you told me! That is a massive step. Instead of giving in to your feelings, though you don't know what is going to happen, you decided to walk in faith with me, and that is a huge victory.

I know you say you panicked MASSIVELY. But you continued to trust me. You felt fear but did not give in to it. That is the very heart of what my book means when it commands so many times (366, to be precise) 'Fear not . . . !'

I know the power of human emotions and the immediacy of events in your life. I know you will *feel* fear. That is what you did when you panicked. But you did not surrender. You did not commit yourself to fear as an attitude. Like a man walking a narrow path through walls of fire, you walked by faith through the fear. You were assaulted from every angle. The enemy sent his agents in a combined attack. But in spite of all you felt, you stood fast – another real victory that makes me want to say, 'That's my boy!'

You also continue to entrust Helen and the children to me. You said they are not my wife and kids. You are right, but only to a certain degree: I am not married to Helen, and the children are not mine in a purely biological sense. But my link to them is much deeper than that. I love them more than you ever could. Anyone who threatens them sends a knife through my heart.

They were all out when Eddie's men threw the petrol bomb. They continue to be under my protection, because that is where you have put them.

Helen's letter is a huge test. Do you remember when I said, 'When circumstances threaten you, take a moment to listen to the voice of my Spirit, who says, "With God, nothing is impossible!"'? My Spirit is still whispering that to you. After you attempted suicide, I told you I would send you back to bind up Helen's broken heart, to work with patience, kindness and thankful love to remove from her the poisoned barbs of rejection and bitterness.

Now is the time for you to begin that task.

Her letter is full of the hurt and pain you have caused. You have a choice: you can respond to it with venom, because the truth she expresses hurts, or you can respond with the love that comes from my heart. You can be steadfast and make it clear that, no matter what she does, you are never going to give up on her. That is what my friend Paul meant when he wrote, 'Husbands, go all out in your love for your wives exactly as Christ did for the Church – a love marked by giving, not getting.'

This is the moment where the battle begins for your wife and family.

The world around you knows almost nothing of sacrificial love. My Son conquered hatred, fear and bitterness at the cross by the sheer power of his love. The only way you can learn that is to allow him to do the same in you. His Spirit is joined to yours. That is why you have victory within you. You are *William*, the true conqueror, because your destiny is linked to his.

So you can do it. No matter what Helen does or says, you can respond with love and patience because my Son, Jesus, has joined his nature to your new nature. So you do not have to give poison in reply to poison or accusation in response to accusation. You won't get it right all the time, but that is OK. When you blow it, confess it and go on. Nurture your faith by reading Jesus' story and receiving his Spirit. You will find yourself being changed. That is the great adventure.

You are not alone. I am with you always, proud to call you son.

Your loving Father in deepest heaven,

GOD

Dear Helen,

What have I done? I've destroyed the only thing worth having – the love of my family.

You're right. We both know it. I've been an animal. A feckless, foul-mouthed, fornicating son of a bitch.

And I know you well enough to know that when you say it's over, it really is over.

I didn't deserve you or the wonderful family you bore me, and I know no amount of persuading or protesting is going to win you over. After all, you've seen and heard my lies too many times before. Why should this time be any different?

I don't blame you. Actually, you've been a brilliant wife: constant and faithful, putting up with all my mess. You're a fantastic mother, the like of which we both know I never had, and I thank God the children at least have you.

I accept your decision (well, I'm trying to), although it leaves me feeling like somebody's ripped open my chest with their bare hands and torn my heart out. But I guess you know that feeling all too well . . .

I'm so sorry, Helen, my love. I know this is too little, way too late – but if there's ever a way you could trust me with the kids again . . . I'd love to . . . you see there's so much ground to make up . . . and I'm different. Jesus has changed me.

I miss you, but more than that I miss the chance to make it up to you. I now know that with God there is always hope, and so that is what I will hold on to. But my prayer is simply this: that one day you, Tom, Annabel and Jack will know that hope too.

I love you and I wish you greater happiness than you have ever known. You deserve it.

Please give my love to our children.

God bless you, my dear, disappointed wife. I am so sorry for the mess of our marriage. I take all the responsibility; you have always loved me, and in return I continually abused that trust. I am deeply ashamed, but I guess at last I've got what I deserve.

All my love,

Billy xxx

PS If there is ever the tiniest ray of light . . .

Dear Billy,

I got your letter.

It took you a whole month to respond to mine. The funny thing is, I might have believed some of the things you said if it hadn't take you so long to reply . . . and if we hadn't spotted your private detective.

When we first realised we were being followed, I thought it must be one of those delightful characters you call a friend – who's now after your hide and trying to kill us. But somehow it didn't feel quite like that, so I confronted him. He didn't admit he was working for you, but he couldn't deny it either. I suppose you must be desperate to do something that stupid.

This is a very quiet area, and people look out for each other; they notice strangers. Plus we had all the neighbours on high alert for anything remotely suspicious. Your little man didn't stand a chance. We spotted him following us when we went out to the zoo with the associate vicar from the local church, who is becoming a good friend and trying to provide a fatherly presence for the boys.

So why were you really in touch, Billy? Was it love for me and the kids? A pathetic attempt at altruism? Somehow that's hard to believe. Or was it jealousy? (Not that there is anything at all to be jealous about – I think I've had enough of men to last me for a lifetime!)

No, you just couldn't help yourself, could you? Fidget the Fixer – that's what your mates call you. It's what you're always trying to do. Couldn't you stop for a moment to think that if you got a private detective following us someone could use them to track us down? I'm sure you wouldn't deliberately put the kids in danger, but you just don't think.

As for all the other stuff in your letter, I really wish I could believe it. But you're right – I've heard so many lies from your lips, and I've watched you lying to others. How can I trust you?

As for you feeling like somebody has ripped open your chest with their bare hands – that made me chuckle. You always did have a tendency towards the dramatic. I'll give you one thing: you've kept up this 'God' thing a bit longer than I thought you would. Maybe it will be a help to you. Let's just hope your God can keep Eddie Fast away from our kids.

And as for your wishes for my happiness . . . I really wish I could hate you and say you've got what you deserve. But for what it's worth, I hope you find the thing you've been looking for ever since I first met you. Whatever it is, we both know it certainly isn't me.

Stay away from us, Billy. The first sign of you coming and we're out of here to an address that even you won't be able to track down.

Best wishes,

Helen

Dear God,

Well, to say I'm reeling is an understatement. I feel like I've just stepped out of the ring having been boxed senseless after three rounds by the great Muhammad Ali. I really didn't think faith and following you could be this hard. As you would say, 'This really is where the rubber hits the road.' I've have never felt pain like this – not even in my darkest moments.

It all just seems so cruel, to get to this point and then to get Helen's letter.

It really feels like I've snatched defeat from the jaws of victory.

But I'm not giving up. I know the old Billy would, and though I'm hurt (my God, that doesn't even begin to describe it) and I can't stand the thought of not seeing Tom, Annabel, Jack and Helen again, I'm not going to quit. But you see, God, with your eyes I now understand what I put Helen through, and if I'm really honest I don't blame her. She's right to be angry. Very angry. But I can't stand it! I guess you reap what you sow, or something like that, as you would say . . . But I'm going to keep praying that somehow this situation can be turned around, and that one day we'll all be together again. It's what I want, and I believe you do, too.

I read in your book the other day about you being the potter and us mere mortals being the clay. Well, look, just go ahead – I'm ready to be fashioned into something more worthwhile. You see, God, you make me want to be a better man. An honourable husband. A loving dad. Someone decent. Such a shame I had to get to this point before I realised it. But I love you, God, I really do. I'm on my knees. Hear my prayers. Thank you.

Billy x

Billy, my son,

When Jesus called people to follow him, he challenged them to pick up their cross every day. A cross is a place of death – not an armchair. The man who commits himself to walk in my kingdom swiftly discovers pain. You live in a generation that flees pain at all costs.

But I want to encourage you – there is good pain and there is bad pain. The pain of those who flee from me is unending and destructive. The pain of those who walk into the firestorm of Satan's opposition is clean, godly pain. That is what you're going through now, the pain of honest commitment to my kingdom.

Remember I said I was calling you to be a hero? Heroes are not defined by easy success, but by the moments of agony when they are at the end of their resources and must drag themselves up off the floor to face once again an enemy who feels unbeatable. At moments like that, heroes get up and get going. Believe it or not, that's exactly what you've done.

I read your letter with immense pride. You said you felt like you had been boxed senseless by Muhammed Ali. No one knows a man's vulnerable points better than the woman he is married to. When she decides to unleash her anger, she can hit him harder, faster and more accurately than anybody else.

You have indeed been in the ring with 'the greatest'. You've taken a real beating. But you have not given up and that makes me so proud. Your great big brother Jesus marched into hell enduring pain, loneliness, accusation and betrayal, but he *never gave up*.

You're beginning to be like him.

I want you to see something. In this letter you have begun to separate yourself from the domination of your feelings. You say that you have never felt pain like this, and you are right. Twice you said you cannot stand what is happening, but then said 'I'm not giving up', 'I'm not going to quit.' You're going to keep praying, believing that somehow this situation can be turned around – magnificent!

You understand why she's so angry and you are accepting it. The old Billy would have made excuses, defended himself and given up. But you truly are a new man. Keep believing, keep praying. I will keep walking with you and working on you.

You referred to me working on humans like a potter works on the clay in his hands. Talk to a potter. They will tell you just how difficult it can be to manipulate and shape the clay. It feels like something alive in their hands, almost as if it's trying to get away.

That's a good picture. When I work on humans, I am working on something alive and too often they *are* trying to get away from me. *But I don't give up.* When they spoil my design, I continue to remake them into the best. I'm doing that with you because I already see the hero emerging, the better man, honourable husband, loving dad, the Billy I've always seen in my heart. And I am fiercely determined that together we will see that man fully emerge.

By the way, you finished your letter by saying, 'I'm on my knees.' It's a good place to be. Too many Christians spend their lives thinking they can do it for me, never realising that actually they never could do it. I don't need their help.

I just need their availability. Stay available. Remember, the place of prayer is the place of listening, not just speaking.

I love you, son, and I am with you.

Your loving Father in deep heaven,

GOD

God,

This is the hardest thing I've ever done in my life, I can't carry on much longer.

Billy

Dear God,

It's not like you to ignore my letters – are you all right? Only it's been a month . . . was there a tsunami or some other natural disaster that I missed that kept you out of circulation? You haven't been banged up like your mate Paul in the new bit of your book, have you?

Anyway, as I promised, I have been going on praying for Helen and the kids. But – as I guess you know already – I do have a confession to make. I'm afraid I hired a private detective to keep an eye on Helen and the kids, and well, the thing is . . . She's started going to church! Which is great, but the bad news is she's also been out with the associate vicar, who's single, horribly good-looking and, worse still, he's been taking my boys to their football practice! What a nerve! I really want to hurt him. This just isn't fair God, it's not what I signed up for. Is it?

I'm doing my best to play with a straight bat, I'm reading my Bible (you know, the Nearly Infallible Version) and I'm praying a lot, but all this is hard to put up with.

Help me make sense of it please.

Yours ever,

William

Dear Billy,

I certainly wasn't ignoring your letter. It may have felt like that. But the moment you wrote, I responded.

However, like everyone who seeks to follow me, you are discovering you have an enemy, and he does not fight a clean or decent war. He is not chivalrous. He fights dirty. There are times when he tries to obscure my response or your capacity to hear what I have said. Even one of my greatest servants, Daniel, was confused when a reply from my throne was held up by enemy activity. There is a war going on, and the enemy does everything he can to prevent my communications getting through.

I'm glad you finally decided to tell me you hired a private detective to keep an eye on Helen and the kids. So you will pray for them, but won't trust me with them – interesting. Have you ever heard the expression 'Eavesdroppers hear no good of themselves'? What you have been doing is eavesdropping on Helen's private life instead of trusting me to deal with the situation. It's the old Billy, isn't it – the Fixer. 'I trust you, God, but I know you're busy, so I thought I'd give you a hand!'

Is it a male thing? No, it's a human thing, driven by anxiety. Here's the biggest test for you: pray, trust me and leave it in my hands. If you spy on Helen, the information you receive will only make it more difficult for you to achieve that dream ending you're praying for. Fear robs faith of its power. Your actions are in grave danger of cancelling out your prayers.

To answer your question – what you signed up for is to trust me and obey me. So here's the one thing you can and should do. Respond to Helen's letter. Write back with humility and faith, and – here's the test – without trying to manipulate her. The only way she is ever going to believe that you are different is for you to *be* different. If you listen to me, I will help you with the right words.

Your loving Father,

GOD

Dear Billy,

Where have you been? More to the point – where are you? I haven't heard from you for quite a while. That could mean you're paralysed by the grip of guilt. Or maybe something terrifying has happened that's left you devastated, struck dumb with fear. Or is it possible that after the events of the last few months you are simply weary? Perhaps you are depressed but don't know why.

You might say to me, 'But you're God! You know what's wrong!' Yes, but I repeat what I said before. What I know is not nearly so important as what you are prepared to honestly tell me. Talk to me.

Whatever has caused the breakdown of communication, be sure lines are still open this end. Whatever issues you face, my grace, love and sovereign power are more than equal to them – however big they may seem to you. From my perspective they are all manageable! Not one situation facing you will defeat you, provided you stay strong in me. It is true that by yourself you can do nothing. But the key phrase is 'by yourself'.

Billy, my son, you are not alone. I am your true and everlasting Dad. At the moment you are not aware of my presence with you. You feel you are alone on a dark road. But I am there as much in the darkness of the night as in dazzling sunlight. All who belong to me go through this at some point. They call out to me like lost children – 'When it's so dark, how can I know you are here?'

By listening. 'Be still and know.' Turn away from the inner turmoil, the swirling chaos of panic responses. Let

go of the repeated phrases of obsessive thought. *STOP*.
Allow your heart and mind to be still, and listen. You *will*
hear my voice. Then you will know I truly am God and
you are in my hand.

Looking forward to hearing from you,

Always your loving Father in deepest heaven,

GOD

PS My enemy is your enemy, and the enemy of all human
beings. He is an expert accuser. He is also a liar – he has
been from the beginning. When you hear a voice inside
you, whispering so closely that you think it's your own
thought, 'I'm just useless – I might as well give up', know
it has been inserted by the enemy as an accusation against
yourself, which you repeat, parroting his words. He is
childishly proud of this gambit. Don't let him fool you.
He has tried it on many others. He is boringly predictable.
Instead, watch for the creative originality of my action.
Much more fun!

God, it's me, Billy.

Thank you for caring. I've struggled to put pen to paper, because when Helen wrote to me saying she and the kids never want to see me again, I just know she meant it. She spotted the private detective I hired, and that's really it. There's no hope. No light.

So I've been busy drinking myself into oblivion. My tongue is swollen from biting it in my tortured sleep, to the point where I can barely talk, and my head has jackhammers pounding away twenty-four seven. My kidneys are aching, and when I piss it's like trying to pass shards of glass out of the eye of a needle.

Frankly, I don't give a toss any more. I may as well be dead. How are you?

Billy

Billy,

What on earth are you playing at? You're acting like a fool. Didn't you read my last letter at all? Didn't you understand what I said about trusting me in the darkness? Didn't you read what I said about listening to my voice and not to the chaos of panic responses?

Why do you think I warned you? I knew what was coming. Right at this moment you can't afford to give in to self-pity. It will paralyse you at a moment when you need to be free and available to act. It's not all about you!

Too often in your life you've run away from difficulties, and especially run away into drink. Ever since you were a child you've been using this kind of response to create guilt in those you wish to manipulate. But a crucial time is coming. Helen and the children are going to need you more than ever before.

You are my son and I am calling you to pull back from the brink, turn around and begin to be the man you are meant to be. Listen to the voice of my Holy Spirit. Call upon the redeeming power of my Son and begin to be the man I have called you to be.

You can do it.

You should know by now that I will not be blackmailed. I rescued you once. But this time get yourself ready. The biggest test of your life is heading your way. The most important resource you have is your vital relationship with me. You must draw on that – or you will fail and your family will suffer. This is more urgent than you know.

You cannot afford to indulge in any more pity-parties.

There is no time for that.

Get ready, because the test is coming. Remember, I still believe you can win this.

Always your loving

Dad/GOD

Helen's mobile to Billy's mobile

Helen: Billy! Billy! They've taken Tom! Eddie Fast's men came. They've just kicked the door in, locked us all in the dining room and sped off. They say they're going to kill him. Said it's payback time. Help us Billy! Help!

Billy: Give me the address. I'm coming now.

Helen: I'm at my brother's.

Billy: What? That's just around the corner! I'm coming now.

From: Billy Fidget
Sent: Today
To: Father God
Subject: Family
Category: RED

Helen called me from her brother's house. I arrived to find the front door hanging off its hinges, and I could hear Helen crying hysterically behind the locked lounge door. I shouldered it, wrapping my arms around Helen and the rest of the children.

'They've taken our boy! Our boy! – and it's all your fault. I hate you. I hate you!' she screamed.

'Where?' I shook her. 'Where have they taken him?'

'They said you would know.'

My mind raced, and then it came to me. Oh my God! Of course – it's my garage. So am writing this in a hurry. Eddie Fast has kidnapped my son and I think he's taken him to the lock-up behind my main salesroom. I'm going there now. Send your angels.

Love Billy

From: Father God
Sent: Today
To: Billy
Subject: Family
Category: Purple

Billy

The angels are there already. And I am there.

Even while you are driving, remember this – my power is released by faith, not by fear. Remember, pinpoint prayer prevents panic. Panic will do you no good now – reject it. Know that I am still in control.

Walk by faith in my peace no matter what.

My angels are released by faith and loving obedience. Get your head and heart straight. Let your spirit fly and see what I will do.

No matter how bad this gets, remember I am still the Sovereign Lord and I am always and forever your loving Dad.

GOD

Oh my dear God.

This is all too much. I got to the garage and was met by two of Eddie Fast's heavies: Mickey 'Two Guns' and Brian 'Fat Boy' Slane. They grabbed hold of me and dragged me inside.

It was pitch black and there was a foul stench of fear. It was awful. They had my boy Tom dangling on a rope above the mechanic's pit, strapped to a chair in cling film so he couldn't move. They'd put a brown paper bag over his head so he couldn't see what was going on.

In the pit were two attack dogs, restrained by ropes. The dogs were snarling, vicious brutes who looked like they hadn't been fed for days, and the ropes were beginning to fray.

Eddie laughed when he saw me. 'So – come for your son, have you? You've got balls of brass, thinking you can just walk in here, cool as you like.

'Would you like to see what we've been up to?'

But I couldn't look. I nearly passed out. I begged them to let Tom go, and in the end they let him down. I wasn't allowed to touch him. He made a grunting sound but I couldn't work out what he was trying to say.

They took him outside – I don't know where – and then came back for me.

I was sobbing. Crying for my boy, and yes, crying for myself. If they could abduct an innocent lad, I knew I wasn't going to get out of this easily.

The only warmth I could feel was in my pants. I was so frightened I'd messed myself. They stripped me naked and Eddie came right up to me.

'You smell awful, Billy. Was it something you ate? Let's have a look at what the fuss is all about, shall we.'

He grabbed my manhood hard, and twisted.

'Is that it? Is that what my wife thought was so exciting? I put it to you that the right honourable member is really a bit of a shrinking violet when it comes down to it.'

I thought of you, God, and of your Son Jesus as the pain seared through my body. I imagined the pain of the cross and wondered if it was something like this.

Then they stretched me out on the bonnet of my Jag. Fat Boy held one leg while Two Guns held the other. They gaffer-taped my arms and legs to the car.

Then Eddie said, 'I won't be a minute. Just got to find my nail gun.'

He came back, fired the gun and the nail shattered my knee. I must have passed out from the pain. And now I'm here in this hospital bed with more drips and tubes coming out of my body than I care to think about . . .

God, please tell me what happened – is Tom all right? Am I alive or dead?

Is this heaven? *Because my knee hurts like hell.*

Billy x

To: Jerry 'Masher' Harris
From: Eddie Fast
Re: Billy Fidget

Jerry mate, I've got a treat for you. You're gonna enjoy it. You know that little toe-rag Billy Fidget? Well, we finally got hold of him yesterday, and we had a good old laugh! I filmed parts of it and I'm sending you a copy.

I laughed like a drain when he arrived. We'd taken his boy, pulled his shirt off him, wrapped him in cling film and suspended him over the pit in the garage. I put two of my pit bulls down there – just for effect. When Billy came it was the funniest thing I'd seen in ages. Mickey and Brian had him dangling between them. When he saw me, I asked him what he thought he was doing there. He didn't answer.

Then I brought him into the garage and showed him his boy. He was crying like a baby and crapping himself. I gave his todger a real good squeeze. I don't think he'll be coming near my missus again. Probably won't be going near anybody's missus – even his own!

Anyway, we took the boy, we gave him his shirt back, and somebody drove him home to his mum – I think. We didn't need him any more. I wasn't gonna hurt him. I've got my standards.

But when it comes to Billy, I had to teach him a lesson. He's got no respect. You can see that. I can't have people dissing me, not on my own manor, especially with me own missus. So I got that big nail gun and let him have one through his right knee. I said 'This is just a warning – next time it won't be your knee!'

Anyway, he was freaking out by now, seeing all kinds of stuff. So I got the lads to drop him at the local hospital. They paid a young boy to go and say there was a man outside who'd had an accident. He'll have another accident if he comes near my missus again! Anyway, Jerry, watch the video – it'll give you a laugh!

See ya,

Eddie

Billy my dear son,

By now you will know that Tom is all right. I protected him from the worst that Eddie could have done. Although he has had a fright, the one thing he knows is this – when he was in real trouble, his dad came for him.

He saw his dad come to the rescue, and because Dad turned up he was sent home to his mum. Your boy is seeing you very differently now. What he's said about what he saw is going to make all the difference to you in the future. Right now it doesn't seem as though there can possibly be any good in this situation. But in years to come, I promise you will look back on that dreadful day in the garage as one of the best days of your life.

I'm proud of you. You won a victory bigger than you have yet understood. Instead of running away from a problem, you went to meet it – and all for the love of your son. Do you see? It's what I did when I sent my Son Jesus to the cross for you, and now you've acted in the same way.

I am so proud of you.

Your loving Father,

GOD

Billy,

Oh my God!
I am so sorry. I've been a real bitch.
I can't believe what you did. Maybe you have really changed
– how else could you have gone into that garage knowing that
Eddie and his mates were waiting for you . . . and knowing what
Eddie's done in the past? You must really love Tom after all. He's
been telling everyone that you're a hero.
I've been such a cow. Can you forgive me?
I'm coming to see you soon. Don't get the wrong idea – I
haven't forgotten it was your stupidity, your betrayal that put us
all in danger and risked Tom's life. But . . . maybe there's some
hope for us after all.

Love,

Helen

Text from Billy to God

Helen's bringing the children and coming to see me in hospital. Which is great, but I look – and feel – awful. And, God, I'm frightened. I really want her back and she's apologised – she feels so close, and yet so far away still.

What should I do?

Love

Billy

PS The knee still kills, by the way.

My Helen,

I wish I'd been a better man. I've caused you so much immense pain through my selfishness. I've been so lost for so long, I wouldn't have known the right thing to do if an angel had stood in front of me shouting, 'This way, idiot!'

I've never really known how to talk to women in an intimate way. Sure, I know how to make them laugh, pretend to listen, nod, look attentive and all that.

But the thing is . . . I've never once let my guard down. Only you and the children have ever got right into my heart. For the rest of the world I put up defences and faked it all very efficiently. I trusted no one except you and the kids . . . and then I betrayed all of you, I am very sad to say . . . so many times I can't even remember.

I can't, you see . . . I can't let anyone in . . . my childhood was so painful. You know I still carry the physical scars of what my father did, but the emotional scars are even deeper. Still, there are no excuses for what I've done . . .

I've been a liar and a cheat, a crap husband and a lousy father. You're quite right to say you want nothing to do with me. Given my track record, who would? But please can I see Tom, Annabel and Jack?

You know I would die for them, don't you?

Do you know I'd also gladly give my life for yours?

I love you so much and I'm just desperate to get back together with you, no matter how long it takes or how hard and painful it is. I'll do anything to make it work.

Anything . . . except give up my faith. This man Jesus came into my life like a hurricane and swept me off my feet. What

I mean is . . . he's showed me a different way to live that has changed me for ever. He got into my hurting place and he talks to me in a way that I can understand.

He knows all about my past and yet he says he loves me. Me . . . the most useless bastard on his earth. And it is his earth. Did you know that, Helen? You've got to meet him. Even if you don't take me back, please meet him. I love you so much and I don't want you to miss the moment.

This could be your time.

He saved Tom – not me. Oh, I turned up all right, but they jumped me, beat me up – I didn't do any good.

And then I saw hands – rough but gentle hands – and these huge nails were being hammered right through them . . . the man's face was twisted and his body writhing in agony . . . he was crying, his body wracked with pain . . . and then the same bloodied hands tore away from this rough wooden pallet he was fixed to . . . and he picked me up and held me and rocked me like a baby until I cried myself to sleep.

And you know what he said to me?

'I feel your pain.'

Jesus!

So, my dear, sweet, beautiful, wronged wife, I will do anything – but please don't ask me to give up the man who saved me and rescued Tom. I can't do it.

I will love you until the clouds fall from the sky.

Always, until my last breath,

Your Billy xxxx

Billy, my son,

I am so glad to know Helen is coming to see you, and bringing the children with her. Think about it – that's very positive. You say you look and feel awful. But that won't be a great shock to Helen. She's seen you looking pretty awful before! On this occasion, the way you look will speak to her more eloquently of your love for your family than any words you could use.

You say you want her back. Don't try to win her back. She is used to you and your manipulative ways. Be real. Be willing to be vulnerable. No bravado, no pretending to be the big man, no self-pity either. Just be yourself, be my son, and know that I am walking with you through every step of this.

A little reminder – I love you and believe in you.

Trust me.

Your loving Dad,

GOD

PS The knee will heal, but will ache occasionally.

Dear Billy,

Thank you for your letter.

When you talk about the way you've guarded yourself and never allowed anyone in, you're not telling me anything I don't already know. I've lived with the pain of being excluded from your life for years. And I'm afraid. I'm really scared that what you're saying will get me to open up to you, and then you'll hurt me again, just like you've always done.

I'm not sure I could take that. I've just begun to move on and now you're calling me back. I love you, so I'm vulnerable. That's what scares me. I've listened to your sweet talk before and without fail you've let me down. Why should I trust you this time?

Maybe you have changed. I hope so. I'm not sure I can take all the stuff you've written about Jesus. If he loves you so much, how come he doesn't seem to love me? I don't get it.

I'll come and see you and I'll bring the children. But I'm making no promises. I might love you – in spite of my longing to get away. I wish I could say I don't love you. But just because I still have those feelings, it doesn't mean I can trust you, or that I ever will.

I still haven't forgotten the danger you put the kids in.

See you soon,

Helen

God,

I'm really confused. If you exist, I thought you would have been on my side.

My husband Billy calls himself a bastard. And he claims you're his best friend. What have I done so wrong, that you love him and don't give a toss about me? And what about my kids? Where's the concern for them? It's all very well for Billy to say you've forgiven him. What about the hurt he's inflicted on us? What about the way he's ripped my life apart and left me crying myself to sleep so many times?

And now he's got you, and you love him, and he's happy. And I've got nobody. So what have I done wrong? I know I ought to be glad that he's happy but I'm not. I'm furious, more angry with you and him than I can begin to say. What right does he have to be forgiven and tell me he's changed? I'm confused.

I'm even more confused because sometimes it looks as though he really has changed. How could that happen? I thought I'd got it fixed in my mind that he was exactly what he said – a lousy bastard, worth nothing. And now suddenly he turns around and starts to be the man I always wanted him to be. But it feels too late for me. I don't know whether I dare trust him again.

And what about you? When are you going to help me? I've worked so hard to do the right thing and it seems as though you don't care. I don't understand – I just feel lost in the middle of it all and I don't know what to do.

If you exist, for Christ's sake (I suppose that's right isn't it?) help me! I don't know what else to do.

Helen

PS I suppose if you don't exist and this letter is pointless then at least there's no one who's going to know how embarrassed I am.

Helen, my dear girl,

It's good to hear from you at last. Several times in the last few months I thought you would cry out to me, but you never did. I know all about what's happened. I've watched over you ever since you were born – even more so since you met Billy. I know about the pain he has given you. I know what he's done and the damage he has caused the children. I know you through and through.

You say I don't seem to give a toss about you. Actually, I love you more than anyone you know has ever loved you. I have been longing to help you but you've never asked – until now. The problem is, people often armour themselves against me because they know by instinct that the closer I get, the more the tears will come. That's because I always come to heal. But to heal I must touch the place of hurt.

So if you will stay open to me, I will not only help you, I will heal you. I will set you free from all the stuff that has made you feel like rubbish. I will release you to stand tall, beautiful and free – as I dreamed of from the beginning. I will take the sadness from your heart and replace it with dancing. Do you remember how you used to dance when you were just a little girl? I'll give that back to you – if you'll let me.

Your loving Dad in highest heaven,

GOD

Hi God,

It's me again. Helen and the kids have just left. I feel exhausted.

Annabel cried when she saw my knee and all the drains coming out of it. They've tried to rebuild it and say I should be able to walk again, but right now they can't guarantee it. I've been told I've got at least six months of intensive physiotherapy, during which time I'll have to walk with crutches and won't be allowed to drive. No more life in the fast lane for me. But you already knew that, didn't you?

Little Jack just shouted 'Daddy', and ran to my bedside.

I could tell Helen was sorry to see me in such a state when she first walked in – but only for a second. After that her beautiful green eyes turned to flint, and it felt like massive steel shutters came down to encase our hearts and conversation.

Tom was full of it, of course, telling the nurses and doctors how brave I'd been and how I'd saved his life – but we know the truth, don't we? my friend?

I've had some lousy earthly role models but I do feel you're like the best friend I never had.

Anyway, there was one saving grace: as she was leaving Helen gave me a hint of a smile and said, 'Don't go disappearing again now, will you? We – I mean the kids – need you.' So it's not all doom and gloom.

But – and excuse the metaphor here – it's not been a walk in the park either!

Love from your pal,

Billy

Billy, my son,

Well done. You didn't try to blag your way through it; you were real. And though it may not feel like it, that was a victory. Your family love you – all of them – but too often you have kept them at a distance with your fast-talking, Jack-the-lad defence. The weakness you feel, you experience as humiliation, but for them it's an opportunity to reach out to a dad they love. Each of those kids in their own way will love you more because of this.

As for Helen, you have no idea how much courage it took for her to smile as she left, and to say what she said. She's a smart as well as a beautiful woman. She knew what she was saying. Keep on praying for her and keep on loving her unconditionally. What she needs to know is that you will love her when she's giving you nothing. Because of what you've put her through in the past, *she will test you*. But don't give up on her. As my friend Paul once wrote, 'Love never gives up.'

What you called love in the past was no such thing. It was a passing attraction, usually a moment of lust. It depended on getting what it wanted. But my love *loves* because it sees the loved one as precious, valuable in themselves. My love goes on loving no matter what the response may be. That's the love I am making available to you. Receive that love for yourself, then pour it out towards Helen and the kids. The more you receive, the more you can give. The more you give away, the more room there will be for you to receive more of me.

I know right now you feel as weak and ineffective as you have ever felt. Let me introduce you to a fundamental principle of life. Paul wrote, 'When I am weak, then I am strong.' Because you feel vulnerable but are drawing on my love and my strength, you are really stronger than you have ever been.

You asked whether you could call me friend. Of course you can. When you became a follower of my Son, you became a friend of his. As my son, he walks with me in friendship – all true dads want their sons to grow to the point where they can be not just father and son but friends together.

So, my friend, this is my invitation. Do what friends do – walk with me, and talk with me as we walk. As we do that you will discover what true love is.

Your friend and Father in highest heaven,

GOD

Hi God,

It's Helen here. Thank you for writing back, and for reminding me of what it was like to be a little girl again.

If only life could be as simple as that now. I feel tainted and weary from a life of living with Billy – stained by his deceitful trysts. Just how many people he brought into bed with us I'll never know, and I don't want to. I'm just glad I haven't got some awful disease or something – and yet in some ways that might be better! At least I'd have some physical manifestation of all the pain he's caused me and the kids.

Isn't it bizarre that I want a badge so the world can see how wronged I've been? I've come to feel like an old dress you get out of the wardrobe once a year, hold up to yourself in the mirror and realise that you'll never ever fit into it again. I know what it is to be paid lip-service, then discarded, and even on occasion silently abused. Sometimes there's nothing quite like the tyranny of silence, is there?

Well, let me tell you this: I'm down but not out, and yes, I want to learn to dance again. Please, please show me how. You seem to have worked some kind of minor miracle in Billy – perhaps you can do the same in me.

Love,

Helen

My dear Helen,

I reminded you of how you felt as a little girl on purpose – not to torment you with something that can never again be true, but to draw you towards a new life where that little girl who used to dance for sheer joy would once again dance as she did . . . but now with even more understanding.

You showed great wisdom in what you wrote. You feel tainted because you *are*. Billy dragged all his adulterous unions into your bed with him, and shared them with you. Every sexual union creates an invisible link, a sort of elastic tie to the other person. That is part of the reason you feel the way you do.

But that darkness does not have to stay in your soul. It can be lifted, and you can be clean again.

There's an issue, though. You say you want a badge so the world can see how much you've been wronged. Yes, that would show the world what Billy is like. It would bring out into the open the way he has abused and misused you. But there's one problem – it wouldn't deal with the way you feel. In order to bring him before the bar of other people's opinion and show him as guilty, you must hang on to his offences against you. As long as you do that, you can never be free of them.

Here is the really hard part. The other reason you feel tainted is because you're clinging on to anger and a desire for revenge.

So here it is – if you are ever to dance again as you once did, free and unfettered, you have to drop the charges against Billy.

You have to forgive him.

My family is a family of forgiveness.

So, dear daughter, can you let go of all of his offences? Drop the chains? Undo the handcuffs – and set him free?

I can hear you say, 'Why should I?' The answer to that is because it's the only way you can be free yourself. Think about it, and let me know how you feel.

Your loving Dad,

GOD

Dear God,

Thank you for writing. So much of what you say makes sense, especially about forgiveness. The thing is . . . even if I could forgive Billy for hurting me, I'm really not sure I could forgive him for breaking the children's hearts. I know Tom thinks of him as a hero now, but then he also remembers that Billy was never there for one single birthday, or any of the parents' evenings at school. Annabel can remember him coming home pissed late at night. Fortunately Jack is mostly too young to remember the temper tantrums when he would throw the phone against the wall and smash it.

Really, being married to Billy was like being a single mum – the only time we were together was when he made it home to bed, and then, as you know, he always brought the ghosts of countless liaisons with him.

So I'm really not there yet. Yes, I can see the change in him, but so far he's been anything but consistent . . . a bit like my own father, really, always looking for the next thrill – whether it was sex in the back of the car with his best mate's wife, or a drunken fumble after closing time with Pat the barmaid from the Constant Grouse. It's a wonder his willy didn't fall off, but there you go.

To be honest, I've never been able to trust any man – but I do trust you. So will you help me, please?

I'm going to take the children to see Billy once a week until he's out of hospital, and we'll try and help him when he's out, but I'd be a fool to risk anything else right now. And the price of forgiving him is way too high – so much has happened.

Too many skeletons in the closet. Oh, don't you just love a good cliché, God?

Anyway I've got to go and pick up the kids from school now. Same as always.

Thank you for caring.

Love,

Helen xxx

My sweet Lord,

I know that sounds a bit corny, but I do love that song by George Harrison – and I love you (in a very manly way, of course).

I'm just writing to say that the doctors are talking about discharging me. I'll have to take it easy at first, and obviously there's a great deal of physiotherapy ahead. The thing is, I don't think I can cope on my own. Of course I'm in pain, but I'm feeling pretty raw emotionally too. I was wondering if you thought, given the fact that I'm unwell, that Helen and the kids might allow me to live with them while I recuperate?

Do you think it's a good idea, or am I being far too optimistic? I'd really appreciate your wisdom on this, Lord.

Yours always,

Billy

Helen, my dear girl,

I like your letters. You say what you mean, and honesty is always helpful. However, can I warn you of the seduction of being noble?

You say that even if you could forgive Billy for hurting you, you don't think you could forgive him for hurting the children. It's something I often hear – 'It's not about me, you understand, I'm hurt on behalf of the others.' That kind of attitude is just as effective at keeping people prisoners, and because it seems unselfish, it's even more difficult to deal with.

Please don't think that, in asking you to forgive, I am in any way suggesting that Billy's actions have been anything but selfish, mean and vile. If his actions were not like that, forgiveness would be cheap and easy. But his actions were utterly despicable. And yes, you are the victim – but you weren't born to live like one. Forgiveness will be costly – but worth it. I want you to know you're forgiven, but you'll never know that till *you* forgive.

You say you like a good metaphor – so do I. Did you catch what I said about handcuffs? When I asked you to undo Billy's handcuffs, it wasn't just for his sake, but for yours too. As long as you have him handcuffed to you, you're as much a prisoner as he is – so now is the time to let go.

About the kids: it'll take time for Billy to build a new relationship with Tom and Annabel. With Jack it'll be easier, because he's so young.

I'm glad you can see the change in Billy. I understand when you say that he's been anything but consistent – and you are right. But there's somebody else involved now, and I'm completely consistent. When I get involved in someone's life I persevere with them to the very end, and I am determined that Billy will become the hero I always dreamed of.

You've never been able to trust any man, you say – but I'm not a man. I am God.

You're right – so much *has* happened. But it's not too much for me. I believe in you; I believe you can come through the storm of bitterness and unforgiveness, and dance for joy once again.

But for that to happen, you'll need to get closer to me.

Your loving Dad in deepest heaven,

GOD

My dear son,

Good to hear from you.

Thousands of years ago, a young poet and soldier called David wrote that every word I spoke to him was sweeter than honey; be encouraged that you are finding similar pleasure in my presence. It is what you were made for. I had to smile when I read that you love me 'in a very manly way, of course'. There's no need for embarrassment. You were made to respond to me with all your heart and love me with everything you've got. You're just beginning to find the reason for existing.

I'm glad to know that you are to be discharged. Physiotherapy will at times be painful. It will certainly involve discipline – not something you've been very good at before now! Face it with courage and I will walk with you every step of the way – literally, every step.

You asked whether I think Helen and the kids would allow you to live with them while you recuperate. I think you should ask them. But your asking has to come from a place of vulnerability. You're in a place that you hate – a place of need. No amount of trying to fix it will work its magic this time. You have to ask, with things you haven't often exercised – humility and truth. And you will have to know that in this situation your fate lies in their hands.

Humble yourself, Billy. Ask for my help and let me guide you in the asking. Trust me. I will help them in answering you.

I'm telling you that it is right to ask. I know part of you is screaming, 'But how will it work out?' All I will say is, you can only try. Walk by faith – each step. You've asked for my wisdom. At this point in your life, this is the right thing for you to do. And courage to do the right thing is always a wise choice.

So there's my answer. It's the right thing for you to do. Just do it.

Your ever-loving Dad in deepest heaven,

GOD

Dear God,

You're so right about everything. I've always worried about being perceived as anything less than a macho man, and yet you know only too well that I have a sensitive side. And yes, of course I feel vulnerable, but it's nothing compared to how I used to feel as a child when my dad came into the bedroom I shared with my sister. That was real fear.

Anyway, now you and I are in relationship, even though it's challenging, I now know that I can call on you anytime and you'll be right there.

That assurance is the best gift I could have, so thank you.

And here I am, humbled. Truly reduced to a limping wreck. All that's missing is the eye patch and the parrot! So I'm going to throw myself on my family's mercy, and hope and pray.

By the way, as I write this I'm remembering the Bible verse that used to hang over the altar of St Ethelred's when I was a kid. I think it was from Micah – it said something about 'walking humbly, loving mercy and acting justly'. It's funny, but just before I go off to sleep at night that verse pops into my head.

Coincidence? I don't think so. So thanks for that, God. I love you.

Billy

Billy, my lad,

Well done for determining that you will go for it and throw yourself on the mercy of Helen and the children.

Perhaps I should point out that there's a huge difference between the vulnerability you feel now and what you felt as a child when your father came into your bedroom. Then you were vulnerable because you were faced with a power far greater than your own, and you were incapable of effective resistance. You were defenceless, no matter what you did or said. The difference now is that you *choose* to be vulnerable. You'll have to abandon the very defence mechanisms that you put in place because of your previous experience. This is a matter of your choice, your free will. And that's why I'm saying 'well done'.

I'm walking with you each step. You say you're limping. I quite like the eye patch and the parrot. But my favourite character with a limp is someone else. Do you remember lying, cheating Jacob? He came face to face with the angel of my presence, my own Son, who took on a human body and wrestled with him. Muscles straining, sweat pouring. Jacob – who had twisted and manipulated his way through life, avoiding every real confrontation – was now face to face with my fatherly love. In his desperate fear of his own brother, he refused to let go of my Son, shouting, 'I will not let you go unless you bless me!'

It was a moment of genuine truth – the first one of his life. My Son asked him his name, which basically means a twister, a cheat. When Jacob forced that hated name through his lips my Son said, 'We're changing your name:

no longer Jacob the twister, but Israel, a prince before God, because you have wrestled with God and won.' And my Son blessed him. But while they were wrestling he had put Jacob's hip out of joint, and so Jacob became a limping man. That's you, my son – Billy the liar and William the conqueror. Like Jacob, you will have a permanent reminder of the days that have changed your life.

As for the verse you remember, 'Act justly, love mercy and walk humbly *with your God*' – those last three words are the vital part. Walk with me, your God, and you will limp your way into the glory of eternity. Just keep going one step at a time.

Oh, and thank you. I also love you.

As always,

Your loving Dad in deepest heaven,

GOD

PS When you can't walk any further, let me carry you. Just don't give up.

Dear God,

When you write to me you always seem to hit the mark. At times it's been painful, but it's always been worth it. Looking back on my life, I now can't imagine how I possibly survived without you. I was alive but I wasn't *really* living.

And as for the Jacob analogy, flipping heck! I know I'll always limp, but I'm no longer crippled by guilt and the dark forces that plagued my head and heart.

And it just feels like things are getting better all the time . . .

. . . like what's happening with the family. It's amazing, but after a lot of lobbying by the kids Helen's agreed to have me stay in the house for a while until, in her words, I get back on my feet – well, she always did have a wicked sense of humour! But she insists that I'll have to find my own place by the end of the month, come what may.

I'm so happy! We'll all be together again – and who knows what might happen? I'll keep you posted . . .

Much love,

Billy

My son,

I'm really glad that you now understand the difference between merely existing and being alive. So few people get that. What made the first human truly alive was that I breathed my life into him. From that moment, he was a living being. He lived as I live. When he turned from me, it was not only a move into darkness out of light, but out of life into death. He died from that moment. Of course, he continued to exist. But he was no longer alive with the same quality of life he had shared with me. The woman who had turned from my clear commands suffered the same fate.

Ever since then my heart has been turned towards the human race, longing to win you all back. So I love it when you say you feel alive. It's because you are now as you were designed to be – in a relationship with me.

Religion couldn't do it. It can only add to the burden of guilt. But now you are alive. As you continue to walk with me, that sense of being alive will grow in intensity within you. As long as you stay close to me it's true that things will just carry on getting better and better.

I'm glad you're amazed – you should be! And you sound suitably grateful that Helen has agreed to have you staying in the house for a while. Stay thankful: she's taking a huge risk. You're right – she does have a great sense of humour. But her smile is rueful and her laughter frightened.

Take your time on this one, Billy. Don't take anything for granted – especially not Helen. Open your eyes to see what an amazing woman she really is. If you can see her and learn to love her as she has longed for all her life, then indeed you never know just what might happen. After all, miracles truly are possible – with me.

Stay in touch,

Always your loving Dad,

GOD

Oh my dear Lord, help!

I've only gone and invited Billy to stay with us, 'en famille' for a month, until he can cope with things – I must have gone stark raving mad!

You see, it's the kids really. Tom was the most insistent, but they all basically said to me in their own highly individual ways that they wanted Dad to stay with us. Tom just kept going on about it, but Annabel really got to me to when she said how if the shoe had been on the other foot and I were the guilty party, hurt in hospital, Billy as he is now would take me back . . . so why won't I do the same for him? And then she reminded me of our marriage vows – 'in sickness and in health' – and I pretended I wasn't listening.

Well, of course I was listening. And finally Jack drew a picture of our house with us all inside and Billy standing at the gate, and he stuck it on the fridge.

That was the final straw. I gave in. So he's coming to stay. And I'm terrified. Terrified of falling in love with him all over again . . .

Please help me. I'm doing the very best I can.

Love,

Helen xx

My dear Helen,

It's always good to do the best you can. But don't you think you might need more than the best you can do in this situation? You say you're terrified – terrified of falling in love with him again. And you're right to feel unsure about going back, because you and Billy need more than you had in the past. His insatiable need for affection and your desperate longing for security clashed and caused so many tensions. Your need for Billy to be reliable, to give you stability, frightened him, while his longing for affection exhausted you. You were two hollow people trying to fill your own needs with each other. It was ridiculous.

Your hearts were made for me, and only I can satisfy them. You're attempting the impossible when you try to provide what I alone can give. Billy has begun to discover that the love I have for him is more than enough to fill the aching void deep inside him. Only this relationship can satisfy his desperate need for love.

What about you, my dear girl? Billy is a new man, but he isn't perfect. He *will* let you down again. He won't mean to, but he'll do it, because like all human beings since the Great Rebellion, he carries within him the virus of selfishness. The safety you long for will never be found in Billy, only in me. My Son said, 'Peace I give you, peace such as the world cannot give.' That's what *you* need. So what about it? Will you let me in to give you the security you long for?

You've done a really brave thing already – invited Billy to stay as part of the family. It's not quite stark raving mad, but it is acting with courage and compassion, and sometimes that can make people a bit crazy! The kids knew what they were doing, didn't they? Bring Dad in. Especially little Jack's picture of the house with everybody in it, and Billy standing alone at the gate.

Here's the thing – that's where I am, standing at the gate waiting for you to let me in. So how about it? Will you let me in? I'm the lover you've looked for all your life. I'm the one you long for. I'm the only one who can heal your heart.

I'm waiting.

Your eternal friend and lover,

GOD

Hi God,

I loved your last letter to me. So direct. So honest. But the bit about being a lover freaked me out. What on earth do you mean? It all sounds a bit kinky to me and I've had more than my share of that, thank you very much!

Love,

Helen x

Helen, my dear girl,

You say you loved my last letter because it was direct and honest. That's the way I feel about you. Thank you for asking me what I meant about being a lover. Remember what I wrote: 'You're attempting the impossible when you try to provide what I alone can give' – or, of course, to get out of somebody else what I alone can offer.

Since you first met Billy you have wanted him to be the lover of your soul, the one who sees into the heart of you and loves you for who you are. Your frustration was that he looked at the exterior and went *WOW!* – but he never really took time to get to know the person inside. There's a longing for love deep inside human beings that nobody but me can satisfy. It's insatiable.

So when people demand that love from another human being, it never fills the emptiness in their soul – no matter how much they are given. Only my love can do that. When my love flows in to fill the human heart, people no longer need to look to a human lover to fill the empty place inside. Then at last they are truly free to be loved by another person.

So there's nothing weird about my love for you. Flowing into every part of you, it frees you from the torment of searching for total fulfilment in a human lover. It releases you to love and be loved.

Sex, you see, was my idea from the beginning. I wanted its heights and depths, its pain and ecstasy, to prepare my children for the reality of heaven. But instead of receiving it as a gift, they make it a god. They make it the supreme value. It torments and disappoints because a weight of expectation is placed upon it too great for it to bear.

The same is true of human lovers. They cannot bear the weight of expectation placed upon them when they are made objects of worship.

Do you understand? I am the heart of all love. All affection flows from me and finds its destiny in me. Relationships between humans are like fragile fibre-optic cables in a telephone system, or the invisible radiations that join the mobile network and depend on electricity to make them work. In the same way, relationships in my creation cannot work without the ever-present, ever-effervescent, invisible influence of my love!

Now let's return to my question. I'm standing at the gate, waiting for you to let me in, because I truly am the lover of your soul, the one you've looked for your whole life. And I am waiting for you to let me in.

Your friend and lover in deepest heaven,

GOD

Dear God,

I'm in! I'm actually back in the family home. It's changed a lot since the fire – Helen has completely redecorated the whole place – and there aren't any photos of me downstairs at all, just in the kids' bedrooms.

What were left of my old copies of *Auto Trader* and *Motor Sport* have been shoved into an old case in the garage. It feels almost like she's tried to eradicate the fact that I ever lived here. It all feels very strange. Helen is polite but she'd make a polar bear look positively warm by comparison.

It's so good to be back with the kids again, though. I've really missed them. And now I know how life can really be, I feel that I've squandered most of their early years through being such an arrogant, selfish idiot. Anyway, I must try not to look back, because I know you don't. I'm on the sofa bed in the lounge at the moment, as the stairs are still a problem. But apart from that I think I'm slowly getting mobile.

I've started to talk to Tom about the whole garage incident, but he can't see the wood for the trees and keeps calling me his hero. If only he knew!

Annabel is a little withdrawn, as you might expect, and Jack is happy to have me in the house – he keeps asking when we can go to the park to play football.

How do I answer that?

I don't know if I'll ever be able to run again ... but you know, don't you? So, God, I'm going to go out (if you'll forgive the pun) on a limb here.

I know you love me and want to see everything work out for those who love you ... so I'm going to pray that one day I'll be able to play football with my little boy Jack. I don't expect to be able to run gazelle-like round the pitch, but just to be able to kick the ball back and forth with him would be immense. God, I'm asking you in faith and believing that with you this is possible.

Thank you, Dad.

Right, got to go now – Helen says she needs to have a serious chat with me. Please watch over us.

Love,

Billy

Billy, my son,

Congratulations. You're back in the house with your lovely kids. And now you have a chance to really make it a home. After all, over the years you lived there before, it was never truly your home. It was just a base. Your home was wherever your wandering heart took you. Your showroom was more of a home to you than that house ever was.

Helen has clearly used the insurance money wisely, taking the opportunity to have a clear-out. Don't interpret that as trying to eradicate you. Treat it as if she is asking, 'Have you really changed, Billy? Or are you still the same double-dealing, lying cheat you always were?'

Don't forget, all those photographs remind her of the days when you would come home, make the kids laugh, flash your smile about, drop a wad of money, then vanish again to be with some other woman. Those copies of *Auto Trader* remind her of how you used your showroom and the apartment above to chase women who were constantly taking her place in your heart.

She's asking you a question, giving you a chance, putting an empty space in front of you, saying, 'Show me the new Billy. I want to see if he's real.'

You say she's polite but seems cold. Have you thought she might be frightened? Scared that once she lets the 'new' Billy back into her heart, the old Billy will betray her again?

You've been offered a gift, a chance to start again, taking the life and love I give you each day to become the new person I've called you to be. So don't squander the gift. Be grateful. Thankful people are never miserable. You're right: you've wasted years in arrogance and selfishness. But don't let those years define who you are now.

Listen to Tom. He thinks you're a hero and that is absolutely right – right that a boy should feel like that about his dad, right in that you really did put your own life on the line to save him. Don't rubbish that, Billy. It was a rare moment of unselfishness. For once you did the right thing, and that's why I sent my agents to make sure you came out of it alive. That kind of faith and courage always attracts heavenly help.

Annabel is taking her cue from Helen. She's being like her mum, watching to see whether this daddy will do what the old daddy used to do, or whether this time he's really come to stay. She wants to be able to trust you and she's watching to see whether she can.

As for Jack, he's my little messenger to you. He keeps pointing you towards the future, asking, 'When can we go to the park to play football?' You ask how to answer him. Try, 'Not quite yet, son, but as soon as I can. I'm praying that my leg will get better and I think God is listening to my prayers.'

You might be surprised by his response. You see, I know Jack quite well. He talks to me regularly and hears my voice when I speak to him, better than anyone else in the family. So you see, you owe a lot to his prayers.

You're a lucky man, Billy Fidget. That's what people say, isn't it? When good things happen to people who don't deserve it – they're lucky. And so you are.

A final word. This conversation with Helen is important, but what really matters is not what she says but the way you respond – remember that. And above all, trust me.

Your never-failing Dad in deepest heaven,

GOD

Dear Mrs Fidget,

You don't know me, but through my father I know about your circumstances and some of what you've had to endure. What I am about to write might well shock and appal you, but as I understand it, you and Billy are kind of estranged at the moment – and I thought what I have to tell you might just help.

You see, I knew Billy when he was a teenager just before his abortive attempt to go to university. He was a complete scallywag – always getting into trouble – and he was also the first boy I ever kissed.

Even now I remember it very clearly. We were in the lounge of his parents' house and he was standing there in his motorcycle leathers (he only ever had a moped), holding his lime-green crash helmet, trying to say goodbye to me . . . sort of patting me gently on the back, and then suddenly there we were face to face, and our eyes met and then our lips for the first time. It was so exciting, but he was so gentle, almost like he was tasting something he never realised had existed before.

Later on, when he explained about his father and the abuse he had suffered, I knew just what that kiss cost. It felt almost holy. Sacred, even.

As our relationship progressed Billy kept looking for greater physical commitment from me. He wanted to go (what did we used to call it?) 'all the way'. Well, one night he got me more than a little tipsy – though I could never figure out how until recently – and he took me. I don't remember it, I was so out of it, but I started to remember afterwards. I'd promised myself and God (oh yes – I forgot to say, I'm a Christian) that I'd save myself for the right man. But in truth Billy stole my virtue that night.

He wasn't violent, but all the same he was like a thief, taking what he wanted. Have you ever lain there afterwards and felt so ugly and used you just wish the earth would swallow you up? Well, that's how I felt. Billy had taken the one thing I had to give that was mine.

I tried to take my own life. I still have the scars to prove it.

For many years my brother has wanted to find Billy and kill him. My father also wanted to, for a time. Then twenty years ago he started to pray for Billy. He prayed that he might realise what he'd done, but also that he would one day know God. My dad is a remarkable man.

And that's why I'm writing to you, Helen. Not to excuse what Billy has done, but to let you know that I, too, I have forgiven him for what he took that night, and for all the years in between. It wasn't easy. It never is.

I guess the reason I'm writing is to ask if you could forgive him too.

I no longer carry the deep anger and resentment that I used to, and I feel happier for it. Healed, even. But we're all works in progress.

I know about what has happened to you, because Billy wrote to my dad asking for his forgiveness. My father wept tears of joy for his prayers of twenty years so faithfully answered.

I would like to be able to weep tears of joy one day for you as well.

I have no wish to hurt you, Helen, but I thought you might like to know I read one of Billy's letters to my father and I could

see that God had softened his heart . . . My prayer now is that
perhaps you could begin to soften yours.

   Love,

   Sara

Dear Sara,

I hardly know how to respond to your letter.

You're right, reading it was extremely painful – and yet, sadly, not all that shocking. You see, the Billy you describe is one I recognise. Over the years he has been that mixture of charming scallywag, sensitive and tender, capable of making you feel like the only woman in the world, but also ruthless, selfish and abusive.

I'm aware that he's changed. At least, it looks like that. But I'm scared. Billy won my heart when I first met him, and he has had it ever since. But when we finally split up, it was such a relief. I didn't have to wonder who he was with any more or ignore the smell of someone else's perfume on his clothes – or in the latest car.

I was developing a protective distance from him. Then came this change. The new Billy did something I would never have believed – certainly the old Billy never would have done it. He risked his own life to save our son, Tom. When I saw him in the hospital – he was injured in the process – my heart just turned over. I realised I'm still in love with him. If I allow myself to slide down that slope once again, I'll be lost in love and unprotected against anything he might do. That frightens me so much.

You see, Billy was my rescuer. He's not the only one in our marriage who was abused by his own father. When we met, he became my knight in shining armour, taking me away from a dad who misused and abused me in every way. Maybe it's partly what drew us together in the first place. We're both wounded people.

What's worse is that when I look back, I realise that although I loved him with all my heart, I was never able to give him everything. What my dad did made it impossible for me to totally trust anyone, ever again.

So you see, when you ask, 'Have you ever lain there afterwards and felt so ugly and used you just wish the earth would swallow you up?' – the answer is yes, many times, with what my father did. Then later on, once Billy got fully into his womanising, it always felt like that.

I think I can forgive him. But after all that's happened, can I ever trust him? It frightens me. What frightens me even more is that God has started working on me. He is softening my heart. Maybe your prayers are being answered! I'm just not sure whether I want it to go on.

Thank you for writing.

Just one more thing – I've never been able to tell anybody about my dad: you're the first person I've ever told. Billy knows nothing about it. I don't know what his attitude would be if he ever found out that I was not the pure girl he thought I was, but horribly shop-soiled goods. Please don't tell him, or anybody else.

Love,

Helen

PS It's kind of a relief to know that at last someone else knows.

Dear Helen,

Oh my word – you poor thing! Thank you for your honesty, for sharing your treasures of darkness with me. I won't tell anyone, I promise. I've been praying for you and will continue to do so.

If there's ever the opportunity I'd love to meet up. In the meantime, if you're happy to correspond, my e-mail address is below.

Love,

Sara

PS There's also someone else I'd like you and Billy to meet one day.

sara.frederiksen@notmail.co.can

Dear God,

I told you Helen wanted a chat, didn't I? Well, I can't quite take in all that she said.

It started off reasonably enough; after the kids had gone to bed she invited me into the lounge, opened a bottle of red wine and then began talking. She told me how she knew all about Sara – that she had received a letter from her in Canada, telling her all about what happened, sparing no detail. And then she said that somehow Sara had managed to forgive me, and was asking Helen to forgive me too.

At this point her voice started to quaver, and her eyes flashed. 'How could you?' she demanded. 'Well, I know how you could, but why did you? Were you that desperate for sex you didn't care what happened to the other party? You're just like my father. You'd take anything with a pulse any way you could!'

I'll be honest, God, I was completely flummoxed by what she was saying, so I asked her what she meant. And that's where it got very messy.

It turns out that her father used to abuse her. Every Friday night he'd come home from the pub, his breath smelling of whisky and cigarettes, hold her down and force himself on her, while her mother lay in bed upstairs, weeping. All done, he'd zip up his flies and fall asleep in his armchair in front of the fire, while Helen would crawl, bruised and weeping, into her mother's bed. They lived in terror of him. There was no one else, and so this dark vile secret has been kept for decades.

Well, they say that light exposes darkness, and that you see everything – every word and every deed.

Helen said that when she fell in love with me I was her knight in shining armour. Her rescuer – the man who could get her out of this mess and be different. Except I wasn't, and I didn't. And over the years I simply made it worse.

Her father's still alive – he's well into his eighties now, and suffers from Alzheimer's, so the bastard can't even feel remorse. Her mum died five years ago.

And my dear, sweet Helen has carried this pain all this time and never told me. Do you know why? Because she wanted to be perfect for me. She wanted to be pure and unblemished. A virgin. And here's the thing, God – despite all the betrayals from her father and from me, she is more decent, kind, loving and innocent in her heart and mind than I'll ever be. Let me tell you why.

The fact she hid all this from me was shocking, but how could I feel upset after all she'd been through? Shocked – yes. Angry with her dad – oh hell yes! But the most astonishing thing happened next.

She looked into my eyes and said, 'Billy, I know you've changed. I can see it. You've softened. Your eyes are no longer like two cold slabs of grey granite. Now they sparkle and shine. You're more attentive and loving to the children than you've ever been, and you have more time for people in general. You care.

'But you scare me, Billy. I can't take another disappointment. Frankly I'd rather die than feel that kind of pain again. So here's what we're going to do. If you really love me, you're going to invite Sara and her father over here, pay for their tickets, bring them to this house, and make amends. I for one would like to thank her.

'Do you know why? Because she's shown me what forgiveness truly means.

'And if you can do that, Billy, if you can step up to the plate and do the right thing, then I'll let you stay here with me and the kids until you're completely healed. And who knows – one day I might even forgive you. But don't you dare mess up, because I'm tired of being a victim, and if you push me I swear I'll destroy you this time.'

Then she got up and walked to the door, and said, 'Oh, by the way – Sara has someone else she wants you to meet. Something about another relative of hers . . .' and with that she went off to bed.

I cried myself to sleep that night, and have been doing so more or less ever since. Tears of remorse, regret, anger, confusion, and sometimes even tears of joy . . . I'm just so happy to be alive – even with all this pain it's better than living a lie.

So that's it for now, God. I'm still standing, but it continues to be an extraordinary ride.

And I am hopeful. I believe that, in spite of everything, somehow it is going to be all right.

Love,

Billy x

My dear son,

I am so pleased that at last Helen has been able to tell you the truth about herself. Sara's letter released her to do it. The anger she felt towards you had hooked into her anger towards her father – grief and anger often work like that. She has carried that burden all her life. So in lots of ways she had to wear a mask, and you never knew the real Helen. That had huge consequences in your relationship.

Anyway, the anger she expressed to you came from a very deep, dark place in her heart. For the first time ever, she has allowed herself to feel that anger and even tell someone about it. Now you know why she fell for you and what she longed for. She saw the hero inside you. You also know why I've consistently told you that that is what you are called to be – her hero.

Yes, you've messed up so far, but it's not too late. It's never too late to recover your destiny. Remember that. It's not too late to put on the shining armour and mount your white horse.

When it comes to her father's condition, it really is almost too late for him. You rightly say he can't remember what he did. That's partly because he buried it and refused to look at it or even admit to it. With regard to the remorse, you would be *almost* right. What he does feel is guilt. Remorse would imply regret; repentance would mean facing and turning from his evil. But he is locked into the darkness and guilt of the past. And because he has never admitted to it, he is almost completely imprisoned. He feels constant guilt, but doesn't know why. It holds him in its grip and torments him. If he dies in his current state, hell will have claimed his whole life.

Helen's mum did feel remorse. She knew she should have done something to stop it, but fear held her in its vice-like grip. Before she died, she brought it all to me. Now she is whole, and she shines.

You understand Helen now, don't you? And at last you know why you always sensed an inner chamber of her heart that was for ever closed to you. I was so glad to hear her tell you she'd seen how you had changed. Hang on to that. Sometimes the onlooker sees more of the game. You can't see how much my love, grace and presence within you have changed you. They have.

In all she said, she was showing her love for you. In the challenge she brought you, she was asking you to be the hero she always wanted you to be. Don't let go of it. No matter how often you might fail, never let go of the determination that you will act with courage as I designed you to.

So do the scary thing. Pay for Sara and her father to come to England and give them enough money to pay for someone else to come with them. That other relative is important. And don't just listen to what she said; listen to what she did not say. Because her underlying script is that she loves you desperately. Now she has seen you changed, you have unlocked a torrent of hope and faith in the future she never dared to have before. It's why she's so scared.

I'm glad to read you are happy to be alive, despite all the pain you feel. It's so exciting that you understand it's better than living a lie. Walk in the truth, my son, every day.

As you let my Son lead you, he, your friend and brother, will show you just how the truth will go on setting you free. Yes, you're still standing. But don't forget I am calling you to advance – deeper into my heart, and into claiming the destiny I've put before you, deeper into love for your Helen.

And a reminder – this is something you know already – trust in yourself and you will inevitably screw it up. Trust in me, walk with me and you will see something amazing happen. You'll find it mind-blowing!

As always,

Your loving Dad,

GOD

PS Deepest heaven is rejoicing over all you've managed to do so far. You are being cheered on by uncountable numbers of angels and saints. You are not alone.

My darling Helen,

I know it must seem strange to be receiving a letter from me when we're living under the same roof. And perhaps stranger still for me to get Tom to put it under your pillow for you to read before you go to sleep tonight. But whatever happens, now or in the future, please always keep it.

First of all I want to say thank you for sharing with me all about your father and your childhood. Thank you so much for letting me into your hurting place. I feel honoured. You are the most lovely and courageous bright shining star of a woman I have ever met.

And I know I have said sorry many times before, but I feel compelled to say it again after all you have revealed to me.

Darling, sweet, adorable Helen: I am so sorry that your dad hurt you, and that I compounded that hurt. You are the most precious woman on this planet. What does the Good Book say about the 'wife of noble character'? Something about being 'more precious than rubies'? Well you are that, and so, so much more. 'There are many virtuous women in this world, but you, my sweetheart, surpass them all!'

I want to be with you for the rest of my life. I want to love you until the stars rain down flaming and glorious from the sky, until the seas are still, until God decides to take me home. I want to woo you at sunset and hold you in my arms until the sun rises to kiss the dawn. I want to wipe away your every tear, and I want to be with you wholly. Properly, for the rest of my life.

So yes, I have written to Sara and her father Haakon, and they're due to arrive next week. I think, though, that you may well need the extra space, both physically and emotionally, so I've booked into the local hotel down the road. It's not glamorous but it'll do. I love you, Helen, and when Sara and Haakon have gone back to Canada there's a very important question I want to ask you.

All my love,

Billy xxx

Dear God,

Oh my goodness – Billy's only gone and done it! He took me at my word, bought three plane tickets, and our Canadian guests arrive next week. Not only that, he also wrote me the most tender and sensitive letter I have ever received. I'm starting to believe him, and I'm definitely believing in you.

You are a God of miracles, aren't you?

I'll keep you posted, but I'm a very real mixture of excitement and apprehension.

It will be all right, won't it?

Love,

Helen

PS Jack has asked me to say hello to you – apparently you two are buddies?

Dear Billy,

I don't really know how to respond to what you wrote. You've said nice things to me before, but only when you wanted something. Now I read your letter and there's a different tone to it. It's like a letter from a stranger, but one that I've known and loved in the past. Yes, you're right: it is a bit weird living under the same roof and writing letters to each other, but somehow responding to your letter with mine feels safer. Don't expect me to respond in conversation at the moment. I don't think I could trust myself.

Your letter sounds as if you mean it, though I am sure I don't recognise myself as lovely, courageous or a bright shining star. Do I really seem like that to you? Nobody has ever said things like that to me before. I really hope you mean it. Perhaps I can dare to hope.

I will say I am glad – as well as a little afraid – that you have provided the money for Sara, her father and this other relative to come over next week. I am even more touched that you've decided to go and stay at the place down the road. That's so thoughtful of you – quite unlike the Billy I used to know.

It's confusing and scary. After giving me all these reasons to hope, don't let me down, will you, Billy?

Yours,

Helen

PS Because I've never had a letter like this before and I might not get another one again, I will do as you ask and keep it – no matter what happens to us.

My dear Helen,

I was delighted to receive your letter and hear how the change in Billy's heart has touched you.

What you see coming through is the real Billy, the one I designed him to be: a genuine hero, tough and tender, strong and sensitive. I have set him free – free from fear, so that he can be a man of courage, and also free from macho nonsense about what it means to be a man. Now he has been released to be tender and sensitive: the man you always needed for your own healing. I am proud of him.

Thank you for asking – yes, it's true that I'm a God of miracles. And I know the miracle you're looking for now – I know you're beginning to wonder if your marriage could work after all. And the answer is yes, it can. Think of it this way: if you allow my Spirit in to join with your spirit, then that will release you to be the woman you are called to be, the beauty Billy has been searching for all his life.

My Spirit in you both will draw you closer to each other. Call it holy magnetism if you like. You see, I am perfect love.

The nearer you get to me, the deeper it gets and the more you draw near to each other. Maybe it's time for you to do that – to open up to me. I'll be waiting for your reply. In the meantime, don't be afraid. Go forward with trust. There are big surprises coming.

Finally, yes indeed, Jack and I are good friends. He's talked to me on many occasions and, even more importantly, he listens to me. Often children can hear my voice more clearly than those who are much older. So please say hello to him from me, remind him that I love him, and tell him to keep listening out for me and looking forward to his fourth birthday.

Relax, Helen. You are in good hands, safe hands – hands that will never misuse you.

With much love from your friend, your true and eternal Father, your real Dad,

For ever yours,

GOD

Dear Lord,

I'm going to go right out on a limb here. You're a father with a son, aren't you? And even though past history dictates that as the sexes go you're probably not to be trusted, I'm going to do just that.

I'm going to carry on trusting you, God.

I'm counting on you to come through.

For once in my life I need a man I can rely on . . . actually, I need more than a man.

I need you. So my answer to your question is 'Yes'. Do come in. Please.

It's weird, but for the first time in my life I feel a strange sense of peace.

Thank you so much.

Love,

Helen x

Oh help me, God!

I've got to go and meet Sara and Haakon at Heathrow airport in just over an hour, and take them to Helen's – I mean, what used to be our house. I'm petrified. I've lost all sense of peace. I'm panicking, my adrenaline is flying around at a million miles an hour and guilt is gnawing away at me. I know you've forgiven me and so have they, but it just feels so very raw and embarrassing. I don't want to do it and yet I know I have to. I must try and grasp the nettle as firmly as I can . . . but I'm dreading it all. On top of it all I've checked into the local hotel so they can all have a jolly good chinwag without me.

I can't remember the last time I felt this vulnerable. Can you?

Help me, Lord. I simply can't do this in my own strength. I need you. Please help me. I'm begging you.

Love,

Billy

Billy,

Calm down. You're not simply a delivery man picking up a package, or a taxi driver. You're my son – stepping into a moment destined since before you were born. When you're driving, your big brother – my Son Jesus – will be right next to you. You are not alone. When you meet Sara and Haakon, I will be there, in you and in them too.

Do you know why you're petrified? You've forgotten who you are. You've moved from a genuine sense of new identity into all the feelings of guilt and panic associated with the man you used to be. Maybe it feels raw and embarrassing because you're facing your past without covering it up and without covering yourself up. That's a good thing. Right?

And you're right – you've got to do it, so you will do it. You feel naked and ashamed. You're not the first to feel this way, and you won't be the last. Of course they'll have a good chat about you. But why assume that's a bad thing? That's just your fear talking.

You asked me if I could remember the last time you felt this vulnerable. The answer is no. All your life you have evaded any feeling of vulnerability. You ran from it every time. You put on your 'Jack the lad' personality, laughing and joking, all the time running and hiding.

Now you've stopped, and for the first time in your life you're genuinely vulnerable. Of course, you're right – you can't do it in your own strength. You won't do it in your own strength. So the only way to do it is in mine.

You begged me for my help. What's the next step? I gave my Spirit to my Son to strengthen him. Wouldn't I do the same for you? You've asked. So what am I doing? I'm giving.

Now, what's left for you to do? Trust that I never break a promise. I am giving right now. There's just one more step – reach out. Receive my power. Take what I'm giving as a gift. It's the only way it works.

By the way, I have a question for you, a very important question. You've asked me to help you and you know that I will. But here's my question – *why should I?*

Here's a clue: it's not what you know, but who you know that counts.

Your ever-loving Dad in highest, deepest and widest heaven,

GOD

PS Don't panic. Trust me.

Dear God,

I can hardly believe I'm writing this. I'm still reeling from it all . . . as you well know!

So I went to the airport to pick Sara and Haakon up, and I'm waiting there at the arrivals gate, and then I see her – Sara, that is. She's even more beautiful than I remember, and I see the gentlemen who I suppose is her dad, and then a young man, and they march right up and the first thing Sara says to me is, 'Hello Billy, it's good to see you', and she kisses me gently on the cheek, like a holy kiss.

And then she says, 'This is my father, Haakon – and I think it's about time you met your son, Victor. We all call him Vic.'

And this Nordic-looking athletic young man with piercing blue eyes looks at me and he says, 'Dad, you don't know how much I've been longing for this day', and then he hugs me, and I fall to my knees, and I'm weeping and we're holding each other and we're rocking back and forth and then Sara and her dad join us and we're all crying and then laughing, the sound ringing round the airport, and my heart has just . . . burst and great torrents of emotion are flooding everywhere.

The police are called because we're making such a scene, and between sobs I try to explain what has happened. But it's Haakon who says, 'Officer, today I have met the father of my grandson for the first time, and my grandson now knows who his dad is.' Well, at this point, even the cops – who can be a hard-nosed bunch – are visibly moved and they arrange to have us escorted out to my car without further ado, and off we go back to meet Helen and the kids.

So I'm driving, and I'm trying really hard to concentrate but all I can do is look in the rear-view mirror at Sara, her dad and this Nordic version of me, my first-born child, Victor. And I'm thinking, *Oh my God, what are Helen and the children going to think? How will they respond?*

And once again the floodgates open and big fat tears roll down my cheeks. I swear, I have never cried so much.

And I'm thinking, *Once Helen meets Sara and Haakon and then sees Victor, any chance I might have had of reconciliation will be gone for ever*, and yet I promised Helen I would fly them over from Canada and have everybody meet. But I didn't know I had a son from that night when I betrayed Sara so cruelly. I knew nothing about any of this.

Where do I begin? And I'm driving and I'm crying and my heart is pounding in my chest and they're all sat on the back seat just smiling right back at me.

Anyway, we pull up outside my house and – well, this is where it gets really weird . . . We're walking up the path to the front door and all of sudden I feel this massive jolt in my chest and down through my body like I've been hit with a lightning bolt or something and my stomach is burning, and as Helen opens the door I fall into the house and hit my head on the hall table and everything goes black.

And these images come at me, big fat ugly grey vultures and black carrion crows, and they're pecking at me, like they're picking over the bones of my body, except it's my soul that's being tormented and I can't move and my body feels frozen and yet I can smell burnt hair and rotting flesh and I'm lying helpless in this stinking abyss and I can feel cockroaches crawling over my body and something slithering around my feet.

And I see images of my life, my wedding day, Helen dressed in white, Lola Amazonian, naked and straddling me, Sara comatose on the bed that evening I took advantage of her, my mother smiling at me and mouthing the words, 'No, Billy, no. That's not the way,' and my father tying me face down to the bed while my sister cowers in the corner, weeping.

I try and say the Lord's prayer and I can't.

I'm fighting to get the word J-e-s-u-s out and it just won't come.

Then it feels like someone's put a huge pillow over my face and somehow every blood vessel that's about to burst, every air sac in my lungs and every last fibre of my sentient being screams out JESUS!

Billy xx

Billy, my dear son,

What a day you had. The heart attack wasn't something I planned. The moment it happened, the enemy did all he could to claim you back. The filth embedded in your unconscious memories came pouring out to drag you down.

But you did the right thing – you put everything into calling out for Jesus. Your big brother came for you – shouldering through the opposition to rescue you from the grabbing hands of hell. They were so disappointed! Even when someone belongs to me they always try to drag them back to the past to stop them from becoming truly free. But the truth is, the moment you screamed his name, they knew they had lost and began to fall back in defeat.

Can you understand now why I encouraged you to take a moment to receive my Spirit? He strengthened Jesus in his lone battle with all the powers of hell in the wilderness. If Jesus finds him useful, maybe you should bear him in mind! It's not enough to ask for the Spirit. You must receive him. He's the key to all the resources of heaven. You've been under lots of strain recently, and everything that happened that day was more than enough to send your systems into meltdown.

The best part of that horrible moment is that all the poison that came out of the woodwork to claim you was driven off by my Son. The power of his blood washed through you, followed by the crystal-clear river of the Holy Spirit. You've had a complete internal makeover.

I'm glad you so love your son, Victor, though he was a surprise. Sara and her dad have done a wonderful job. He is a fine young man, and a credit to their faith – and you may have picked up by now that Helen dotes on him. She and Sarah are getting on like best friends, as if they'd known each other all their lives.

Have you picked up on all that's been happening while you've been in hospital? Your kids have been discovering their Canadian grandad. Tom has been taking him down the park, demonstrating his football skills. He can't quite understand why his new grandad keeps calling it 'soccer', but he's getting used to it. Annabel quickly became accustomed to being 'Princess' and that's the way Haakon treats her. Little Jack simply loves him. He senses Haakon has my heart.

As for Victor, your kids are just awestruck. They have what you never had but always wanted – a big brother. I've said it before, Billy, you're a lucky man.

I've poured out my goodness on you – goodness you don't deserve. And I will keep on doing that because I love you, and it's such fun.

By the way, you didn't answer my question. Have you thought about it? You've had a bit of time in hospital. You asked me to help you and I asked you, 'Why should I?' Let me know what you think.

As always and ever,

Your loving Dad,

GOD

Dear God,

Thank you for writing.

I had this weird dream where I was lying in bed and everything was brilliant white. There were hundreds of scarlet tubes coming out of my body, like veins or arteries, and they were being held by what looked like an angel. He didn't hold them tightly, but rather like the reins of a horse, just lightly in his hand. In his other hand he had a small white computer whose contents he appeared to be scrolling through. And every time he stopped to look at something, I would feel a small ache in my heart, and he'd smile and say, 'Taken care of.'

His face looked so peaceful, without a hint of malice, and as he looked straight at me I saw him pull the tubes slowly out of me. Each time he did so my body gave a tiny shudder.

When he was finished I just lay there, exhausted.

Words aren't adequate to describe how I felt; the closest I can get is that it was an overwhelming sense of perfect peace.

When I woke up, nobody was there, and there was no sign that anything had happened – except a blood-red rose that had been placed carefully in my hand while I was sleeping. It had pierced my skin ever so slightly.

I wept. I cried for the fact that I was alive and could still draw breath.

I cried because I was free from the pain of the past.

And then my family came in to see me, and I looked at Sara and Helen, and it was as though they were sisters. They were that close. I guess they were sisters of mercy. Related by heartbreak. They came and sat round my bed and prayed for me and I just thought, *What hearts do these women have?*

And then I knew. They have *your* heart.

You asked me why you should care or do anything for me. It is simply this.

Because you love me.

Here I am, forty-seven years old, finally realising that you, Lord God, love me.

Not only that, but I am worth it.

I am worth it, Billy the Scum Bag is worth it, because you are my Dad.

I love you God. I will be in touch soon.

Billy

Billy,

Well done – you finally understand the reason that I should help you. It's not just that I love you, though that is enough. But you're my son, and I am your Father, your Dad. Now you've got that, I'd like you to take a moment to look back. See how things have changed since you first wrote to me. Would you want to go back to the way you were?

Then you thought you were living the life of Riley. But how often did you drink yourself into a stupor just to avoid the ache inside? And the women: you using them, them using you. Nothing eased the pain or stopped the sense of emptiness. There was a reason you reached out to me. Haakon was praying for you. I said it before: his prayers formed a slender but immensely strong line of grace from me to you.

Now it's your turn. There are millions who live with that aching void inside. Watch out for them. Little things will tell you when a person is beginning to sense their need for me. You might be surprised to know that one of them is an old acquaintance of yours – Eddie Fast! Remember the old saying, 'The best revenge is to win the offender.' Just think about it. And think about this, too: if I'm your Dad and you're my boy, then you're going to grow up to be like me – a real father. Not just to your kids, but to many others who are lost and fatherless. My heart goes out to them, and because I'm your Dad, yours will too.

Enjoy these next few days; I haven't finished with my surprises!

Yours always,

Dad

Dear God,

I guess you're my heavenly Father . . . in which case, this is the first time I've had a relationship with a father who didn't hurt me. A father who is kind and benign, perfect in every way. So I am going to call you Dad now as opposed to God – is that OK? I could call you God but you are my Dad, and that's the thing really.

And *I* am a father – yes, Lord, I am a father to four. What a surprise! Victor by name, Victor by nature. Gosh, what a handsome young man. Victor, *my* son. And he is yours as well, Lord; what a credit to Sara who raised him and brought him up in your faith and your truth. What a privilege to know him.

And I am amazed that their family and my family all get on so well. Frankly, God, it really spooks me – I am the one here feeling like the outsider. And yet they're all fruit of my loins, for want of a better expression.

Everyone's connected through me, but what's going on?

It doesn't make sense. There's Sara and Helen, acting like they were separated at birth. My kids are all getting on with each other, and what's more, they all adore their new big brother Victor. Haakon is like an extra grandfather . . . it's going wild, and I'm feeling a little left out here. What can I do?

Help me, Dad,

Love,

Billy

161

My son,

How great to hear from you, and to hear you call me Dad with such assurance. It's taken long enough, but now is the right time for you to learn that that is who I am, eternally. It's the most fundamental thing about me. I am a father before I am anything else. That is why Jesus is so important to me and to you – because I reveal myself through him. He is my Son, I'm his Dad, and together we walk through history in companionship with the Holy Spirit, who reaches out from us and touches the whole of creation – every particle.

Your question – if it's OK for you to call me Dad – is almost superfluous. Of course I don't mind! It is what I am, and it's why I sent Jesus to die, to enable you to become a vital part of my eternal family. So you've learned at last that you are my son because I am your Dad, and now we can really start to explore the destiny I have for you.

When you say that Haakon is like an extra grandfather to the children, I'm so glad. They never knew your father as Grandad. Haakon has become a true father to you, and so he is their true grandad. He will be more significant in their lives than you could ever have imagined. I have filled the gap – not just for you, but for your whole family. The repercussions will be huge – and very positive.

And you'll be surprised by all I do as I draw together your four children and create one family. It is what I love to do, the thing that drives me in the whole plan of salvation for the human race – to draw them all into one great, glorious, laughing family.

You'll be up and about soon, looking to do what you usually do – running round faster than thought can go before you. So take some time first to sit and be really still. Receive my Spirit, the one that makes me real and makes your big brother Jesus truly accessible. We will never desert you.

Your loving Dad x

Dear Dad,

Well, my head is aching and throbbing, just so much information I don't really know where to begin. Let's try and work with this. Of course, you know all about it, because you're so flipping clever.

So Haakon comes to see me and he says he has something to share. It turns out that Helen and Sara were talking about their favourite childhood haunts, and Helen told Sara that she wanted to take her somewhere beautiful, a secret place that she shared with her mum, who used to take her there all the time, though she never knew why. It's by the banks of the River Chess and there's a bridge, a bit like Monet's *Bridge at Giverny* apparently. Helen said it's such a beautiful, serene place, she used to love going there when she was a little girl; she'd splash around in the water, and try to catch the baby mirror carp with her net. Later on she used to take boyfriends there . . .

Anyway, Helen decided to take Sara there, and as soon as they arrived Sara got all excited and said that she knew the place – there's a picture of that exact scene that her father painted, which hangs in his lounge and has done for forty-two years. Not only that, but Sara said the woman in the picture looks a lot like Helen!

Apparently they stared at each other, and then it slowly dawned on them and Sara said they needed to go and talk to Haakon.

Well, old Haakon was asked a hundred difficult questions that morning, but to his eternal credit he didn't duck out of any of them.

It turns out that in the swinging sixties he came over from Norway on his way to Canada to enjoy all that England had to offer: the Beatles, the Stones – all the happenings. He was a devotee of *Oz* magazine and an avid reader of the *NME*, and he used to go and see all the bands. One day he met an exquisitely beautiful woman in a shop on the King's Road and they had a bit of a thing – it was the era of free love. You know, all that stuff about, 'Turn on. Tune in. Drop out.'

Well, that woman was Helen's mother, so what I'm saying is that . . . not only are Helen and Sara half-sisters, but all the beatings and abuse Helen suffered at the hands of her father – well, it wasn't her real dad at all. And he knew. That's why he was so cruel to her for so long.

So now, wrap your head around this one.

Helen and Sara have the same father, and Haakon could pray for me because he knew what it was like to make a mistake and leave a child behind with all the hurt and wreckage of somebody else's life.

So, the other night, I'd finally got home from the hospital and what's happening? They're all going at it in the lounge. Haakon is begging Helen's forgiveness for all she had to endure, and Helen's just saying, 'Dad! Dad! You're the dad I always wanted, the dad I always needed, my Daddy, our Daddy! Oh my God!' And once again they're all on the floor laughing and crying.

Dad, God, you have to know that I'm just totally blown away by all this stuff.

But I know – because of what you've already done in my life – that you can and will unravel this. And I know you can and will bring harmony. I know you are the God of all healing and comfort, the worker of miracles, but I've got to tell you Dad, God, whatever, I can't wait to see what you're going to do with this one!

Love,

Billy

Dear Billy,

What do you mean, you can't wait to see what I'm going to do? Everything that's been going on is evidence that I've been unravelling all this already – busy behind the scenes, carefully crafting each moment, even factoring in your own stupidity at times. I know exactly what I'm doing. All you have to do is trust me, and continue to follow the guidance of my Spirit. There has been so much healing over the last few days, and it will continue.

In the meantime I seem to remember that you said you had a very important question to ask Helen. Perhaps sometime in the next few days you should arrange to be in a situation where you can ask her that question. I have a feeling that the rest of the family would really like to hear her answer.

Can you feel what has changed?

You're moving out of the darkness into the light; out of a deep, dark forest of confusion towards open sunlight and a clear way forward. There is so much ahead of you. Do you realise that all heaven is waiting to see what will happen with you and your family?

One wise man described it like this: 'The angels are standing on tiptoe' – and they are. Not only do I love you, but you are loved by the whole community of heaven. The reason is simple: it's now your true home, the place of your origin. Your real birth certificate is now on record in heaven.

So don't be afraid to step forward. Your destiny is not just about what happens on earth, but what happens eternally, in heaven. It's a solid and absolute truth that the best is yet to be.

Always your loving Dad,

GOD

Hi Dad,

Well, they do say that home is where the heart is, and now my heart is with you I feel like I've finally come home. And, complicated and confusing as the journey has been, I know that you are steering this ship. You're the good captain, and there'll be no mutiny on this vessel. I just want to serve you, as best I can.

I had a meal with Haakon the other night. I'm still trying to get my head round the fact that he's father to Sara and Helen as well as grandfather to Tom, Annabel and Jack, besides Victor.

We celebrated all we'd been given, even though it's been a tortuously long journey. But strangely it's also been full of the most glorious presence that life can give.

Helen's discovery that the man who beat her was not her real father, and that she has an earthly dad who loved her and missed her, is a gift for her to slowly unwrap. That she also has a sister and a brother, and for them to realise that they can love each other, is another remarkable voyage of emotional discovery.

And yet it is strange that back in the time with Sara, when I did all that stuff, we didn't know that you were in the midst of it all. It's so good to know that it's forgiven and that I can feel clean – I've never felt that before!

You kept your promise. You've done good to me, just like it says in your book. You've restored me – and the rest of us. Now my dream is that we will do our best to love you, and live like we mean it.

I'd like to be one of those people who change the world.

I read about Mother Teresa recently. Somebody once said to her that surely what she was doing was just a drop in the bucket in terms of all the pain and suffering in the world. Her response was to say something like, 'But the ocean is made up of single drops.' I love that.

I've experienced so much compassion and grace from you and the people I've wronged – how can I not respond in kind?

By the way, I've got a date with Helen. I'll keep you posted.

Love,

Billy

Billy, my son,

I'm glad you've grasped that you have a home for eternity. Now what you need to get hold of is your destiny as a citizen of heaven who is truly at home on this earth, demonstrating my love to ordinary people.

You know what I mean by that, don't you: leading a life of integrity, showing genuine love, helping and serving others – being a man with the guts to actually stand up for what he believes.

I want you and your home to become an outpost of heaven, so that people encountering you sense the atmosphere of another realm. I want it to become the kind of place that makes people who haven't yet been found by me feel homesick for me.

This is your destiny and purpose. Now perhaps you understand why I've gone to so much trouble to bring your family together, with all its messed up and complicated history. There's nothing on this earth so badly broken that it cannot be fixed when people allow me to get my hands on it.

I'm glad you really want to put me first. Let me warn you, however, there will be times when you don't feel like that – and in those moments I'm going to ask you to trust me and do what I ask anyway.

There will be tough times too, but I'll be there, walking with you every step of the way.

And of course I'll be there on your date with Helen. Don't try to fix anything. Just relax, be honest and be yourself. That is what will win Helen.

Your Dad,

GOD

Dear God,

Well, as you've no doubt known all along, I have a sister called Sara. And although it was such a shock at the time, I'm just excited to have a sister, a brother and a real father. It's out of this world.

So the man who brutalised me wasn't my real dad. I've got a loving father, and for us to be reunited . . . you know, it's just perfect choreography. Now we can all learn this new dance you've given us. We're dancers with bruised knees but light hearts.

There's one other thing that I am a bit worried about . . . Billy's asked me out on a date, and I think I know what's coming. And I think you know just how I'm going to respond. Don't you?

I love you, my heavenly Father – you're different from all the other men I have ever known in my life.

Thank you for that.

Helen xx

Dear Helen,

How I love you, my daughter. Beautiful, intelligent, courageous, strong – and now a woman who has my Spirit within her. That may give you problems from time to time! You are feisty. I made you like that, but sometimes that feistiness needs to be tempered with gentleness, and so you may find my Spirit a bit annoying. One of my best friends once called him 'the Celestial Interferer'.

I know what's in Billy's heart and, yes, I know what's in yours, so be at peace. Turn away from anxiety and trust me. I'm still somebody who believes in romance in spite of everything that can go wrong. I love a story that finishes with those wonderful words, 'They all lived happily ever after.'

For the avoidance of doubt: I love you, my dear daughter. As ever, your Dad,

GOD

My dear heavenly Father,

So much has happened since we came to England, as you know. I was frightened – so scared I almost didn't come. But I had to face my fear, I had to face Billy, and I knew he had to meet Victor.

What I was not prepared for was to discover so much about Dad. I thought I had a really wonderful dad, and I did. He loved me, was faithful to his wife, built us a secure and solid home. I never saw him without feeling that safety wrapped around me. Sometimes he seemed remote, even stern – reserved, I suppose; but now I understand why, and since we've been here I've seen a new side to him.

For so many years he lived with pain and guilt, carrying a burden that no one but you knew about. Once we asked him about the painting, it was as if he was relieved to be able to tell the story. Tears were in his eyes as he asked us to forgive him. Then he told us the whole story of how he met Helen's mother.

He was a lovely dad before, but now he is so free. He smiles much more. It reminds me that nothing is so heavy as the burden of guilt. Now that he's confessed what happened, and been assured that we forgive him, he's a man whose spirit seems to dance.

I always loved him, but now I love him even more. I guess in all this he has become an even better portrait of your love. I see in him something of what I feel from you; I see your heart in him. I don't think anyone could be paid a greater compliment than that.

Scared as I was to come, I'm so glad I did. And I have a sister. I can't tell you how glad I am to write that; I always wanted a sister, and now I have one. I really can't get over it.

Are you always this good to everybody? And this is only the beginning of what you want to do with our family, isn't it?

It's just the start of the adventure – thank you for inviting me to be part of it.

Your loving and grateful daughter,

Sara xxxxx

Dear Sara,

I'm so glad that you've seen the dance that is in your father's heart. The truth is, you are now going to see him laugh more than ever before. You'll see the real Haakon – the young man who left Norway and came to London, bright, bouncy, randy and very happy. He was one of the sunniest people that many people had ever met.

Then he learnt about the birth of Helen, and guilt began to close in. After your birth he thought he had a new start, but then your mother died. It was the beginning of his time in the shadows and the cold steel rain. Now the shadows are lifting, and you are going to see your father as he is meant to be.

You're right, my daughter: the adventure is just beginning. Thank you for having the courage to be part of it.

Always your loving Dad,

GOD

Dear God,

Well, I asked her. I took my favourite red open-top sports car from the showroom, I made up a picnic, I took a bottle of her favourite wine, and I drove her to our special place, Sunshine Ridge – where I first kissed her. I carefully laid everything out on the blanket. At first we sat silently and she seemed nervous as she sipped her wine, but after a while we both relaxed.

Then just as the sun went down I told her that she makes me want to be a better man, and she looked at me with her soft green eyes and said that I *am* a better man. She said I'm not the same man she married, but that I'm different, that I've had surgery on my soul.

Tears were streaming down our faces. I held her close to me and whispered in her ear, 'Would you marry me again?' And she said yes! Then we held each other in our arms and lay down on the blanket.

We celebrated all that you have given us, and all there is for the future.

I remember singing hymns about your greatness back when I was a youngster at St Ethelred's. Well, Dad, now I really know how great you are. I've seen it.

Love

Billy xx

God, God, God, God, God, it's me – Tom! I know we talk to each other now and again, but I thought I'd write you a proper letter.

Guess what? I know you already know – you do know, don't you?

You know Mum and Dad are back together again, and they're going to renew their wedding vows – they're going to have a celebration of their marriage and it's going to be fantastic!

You're the coolest. By the way, Annabel and Jack are also going to write soon.

Love,

Tom

PS Thank you so much for answering my prayers. We can all be happy now.

Billy, my dear lad,

Well done. Brilliant stuff. Now we really can begin!
Your loving Dad,
Always,

GOD

THE BEGINNING